THE GENTLEMAN'S POCKET KNIFE

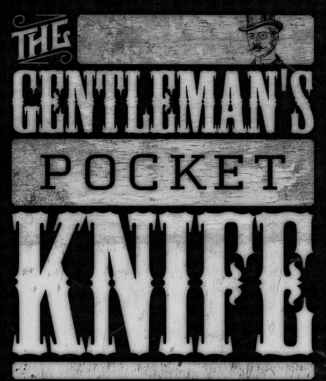

HISTORY & CONSTRUCTION OF THE WORLD'S MOST BEAUTIFUL MODELS

STEFAN SCHMALHAUS

Schiffer Publishing Ltd

4880 Lower Valley Road • Atglen, PA 19310

Copyright © 2018 by Schiffer Publishing, Ltd.

Originally published as *Gentleman-Taschenmesser: Geschichte, Technik und die schönsten Modelle aus aller Welt* by Wieland Verlag GmbH, Bad Aibling © 2014 Wieland Verlag GmbH

Translated from the German by Ingrid Elser

Library of Congress Control Number: 2017953854

Cover design: Justin Watkinson
Interior design: Matthew Goodman
Photo on front cover: Stefan Schmalhaus

Type set in Trade Gothic LT Std, Berthold City & Minion Pro

ISBN: 978-0-7643-5498-4
Printed in China

Published by Schiffer Publishing, Ltd.
4880 Lower Valley Road
Atglen, PA 19310
Phone: (610) 593-1777; Fax: (610) 593-2002
E-mail: Info@schifferbooks.com
Web: www.schifferbooks.com

For our complete selection of fine books on this and related subjects, please visit our website at www.schifferbooks.com. You may also write for a free catalog.

Schiffer Publishing's titles are available at special discounts for bulk purchases for sales promotions or premiums. Special editions, including personalized covers, corporate imprints, and excerpts, can be created in large quantities for special needs. For more information, contact the publisher.

We are always looking for people to write books on new and related subjects. If you have an idea for a book, please contact us at proposals@schifferbooks.com.

"Then I resolutely unfolded my pocket knife and cut off a button on my shirt (at the wrist: she is sewing at the moment, and this brings us closer together)."
—Arno Schmidt, *Das steinerne Herz (Heart of Stone)*

Contents

Foreword

Our grandfathers still knew: a man is not dressed properly without a pocket knife. The pocket knife once belonged as much to the basic equipment of a gentleman as his hunter watch. It served for the small daily duties, and even though it didn't save any lives, it saved a situation often enough. Even today, the intrusion of the analog into our digital everyday world occasionally needs a sharp tool. No app, regardless of how cleverly it is programmed, can open a blister package, peel a pear, or cut off a thread from the seam of our jacket.

But which pocket knife is worn by the man of the world? The prevalent gentleman's guidebooks ignore this practical utensil. The book in your hands aspires to close this gap. It ought to give insight into the fascinating history of the pocket knife to the interested layperson and to give a representative overview over the models available in the market. In the foreground are not the technical details but the cultural heritage. It is a photo book and a book to read filled with history and stories.

The sixty pocket knives chosen are timeless in the double sense of the word. They have a classic design which lasts beyond any fashion. And they are—given sufficient demand—hopefully still available in the near future. Some models have been on the market for more than a hundred years without much of a change. I deliberately abstained from introducing handcrafted individual pieces and rare collector's items.

Like a watch or a fountain pen, a pocket knife can also be an expression of the personality of its bearer. Regardless of whether it's industrially manufactured or in a small series made by hand— the market has the fitting knife for every taste and wallet. A good, stylish gentleman's pocket knife doesn't have to be expensive. A Victorinox with Alox handle scales—just to mention one example— is affordable, suitable for daily use, and above all looks *chic* as well.

This book would not have been possible without multifaceted support. I want to especially thank Ryan Daniels (Queen Cutlery), Achim Gronauer (Friedrich Olbertz), William O. Howard (Great Eastern Cutlery), Henning Ritter (Hubertus), and Guido Schiesen (Robert Klaas) for their professional help. Caroline Wydeau deserves my compliments for the creative design of this book. Hans Joachim Wieland, my publisher, has my gratitude for his trust and his patience.

Stefan Schmalhaus
Krefeld, Germany, October 2014

CHAPTER 1

DEFINING AN EXPRESSION

What Is A Gentleman's Pocket Knife?

Gentleman's pocket knives form a group within the category of pocket knives, but there is no definition with clear outlines. "You know one when you see one," is a commonly used formula in the Anglo-Saxon language area. Here these knives are usually called "gentleman's knife" or "gent's folder." Americans also love to use the expression "Sunday dress knife," which points out two characteristics of this knife type: the gentleman's knife fits with fine dress and is also accepted socially at places where knives usually appear strange.

For very flat constructed pocket knives, which have a small secondary blade and often an additional nail file, in Germany the expression "*Herrenmesser*" is commonly used, although it sounds slightly outdated. The classic representatives of this knife category are already long out of fashion. Many companies in Solingen once produced them in large numbers; they were also favored as an advertising medium.

In their simplest version these knives have handle scales of metal or plastics, high-quality models are provided with stainless steel handles

and artistic guilloche. A special variant of the Herrenmesser is the group of so-called Toledo knives. Their embossed brass handle scales imitate a damascened technique cultivated in the Spanish blade city Toledo. Today they are only available as collector's items or—more commonly the case—as more or less worn-out knives found in attics.

Though its small-format construction is a widely used criterion to distinguish gentlemen's knives from other pocket knives, it can only be used with restrictions because size and weight are relative. Whoever has a glove size of eleven will appreciate every additional centimeter of handle length and rather cope with a few additional grams in the pocket of his jacket.

A gent's knife distinguishes itself primarily by its decent design. Its appearance is self-effacing, stylish, elegant; it can also be luxurious and sometimes playful. At the opposite end of the spectrum there is the tactical folder which has to be up to the hard requirements of situations occurring during police or military missions. Admittedly, the transition between the extremes

▶ **THREE-PART KNIFE OF SOLINGEN:** gentleman's knife by Robert Klaas with embossed brass scales (Toledo style).

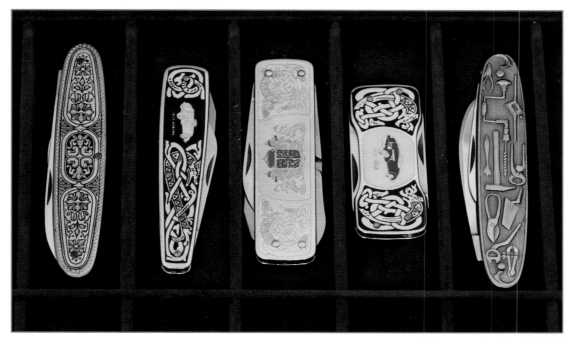

▶ **OLD SCHOOL:** classic gentleman's folders by Robert Klaas, EKA (three models) and Carl Schlieper.

is smooth. There are border crossers among the knifemakers such as Ken Onion from Hawaii, who likes to call the models of his occasional excursions into the gentleman's province "gentleman tacticals." Some modern Italian pocket knives, too, connect noble design with a restrained aggressive note.

The large bandwidth of the currently available gentleman's knives can be roughly divided into traditional and modern shapes. They are mainly distinguished by the choice of materials and design. Stag, bone, mother-of-pearl, and precious wood are decorating the traditional type. Materials such as titanium, aluminum, or carbon fiber are favored for modern gentleman's knives. The famous red plastic look of the Swiss Army Knife is—despite its widespread distribution—rather an exception. In the luxury segment of traditional as well as modern gent's knives you can find all kinds of exotic handle materials from mammoth tooth to

dinosaur bones, or even iron from meteorites.

While the classic Stockman pocket knife today doesn't look different from the ones a hundred years ago, a lot of innovations from other areas of knifemaking have found their way into the technical repertoire of present-day gentleman's folders. Modern locking mechanisms, opening aids, or powder-metallurgical blade steels are common practice. Even a classic such as the French Laguiole knife is now available as a single hand opener with arresting blade.

Finally, I dare to give a short answer to the question raised in the heading without claiming it to be a definition: a gentleman's knife is a practical pocket knife which has, depending on the tradition, one or more blades. In addition, because of its self-effacing, elegant appearance, it can be worn and used in almost all everyday situations without causing alienation.

▸ **SWISS POCKET KNIVES:** these useful little aids are the low-cost versions of a gentleman's knife.

CHAPTER 2

THE HISTORY OF POCKET KNIVES

The Beginnings of Pocket Knives

It was a long way from the stone-age hand ax to the modern hi-tech folder. Over millennia the edges created by the fracture of flint or obsidian were the sharpest blades humankind knew. The first primitive knives were created when stones were attached to handles of wood or bone by means of animal sinews and plant glue. With the advancing mastery of metal treatment it became possible to manufacture knives with blades of copper, bronze, and later on of iron, which already came very close to our modern image of a knife.

It can't be determined for sure when the first knives with foldable blades were created. One of the oldest finds stems from the archaeologically important Hallstatt burial ground, in the Salzkammergut, Upper Austria. The folding knife, dated to the late Hallstatt period (600–400 BCE), has a blade of iron and handle scales from ornamented bone plates.

Several finds from Roman times document the distribution of simple folding knives whose blades were folded into a handle of metal, horn, or wood. From the third century, an extraordinary folding knife with several parts has come down to us, which looks like an early version of a Swiss Army Knife and probably served as the travel utensil of a wealthy person.

The farmer's knives with foldable blade known from the Middle Ages had a tang prolonging the blade, which made opening the knife easier. When the knife is open, the tang rests on the handle back and is enclosed by the hand. The company Svörd of New Zealand still produces such simple knives today.

Nevertheless, all-purpose utility knives with fixed blades were the most commonly used knives from the Middle Ages to the modern era. Men and women wore them in leather sheaths at their belts—quite often in combination with a spoon—because during the Middle Ages it was common that the guests brought their own cutlery to a shared meal. Still in the sixteenth century, reports Erasmus of Rotterdam, urban guest houses were only sparsely equipped with dinnerware and cutlery, so it was recommended to always take a knife with you when travelling.

The history of the modern pocket knife started in England and France in the seventeenth century. The most important innovation of this time was the invention of the back spring—called "*ressort*" in French. In the technical sense, this is no real locking mechanism. But the spring, which holds the blade under tension when the knife is in open position, made handling more comfortable and secure.

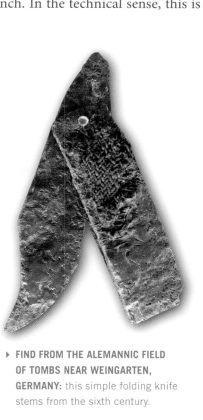

▸ **FIND FROM THE ALEMANNIC FIELD OF TOMBS NEAR WEINGARTEN, GERMANY:** this simple folding knife stems from the sixth century.

▸ **VIKING KNIFE OF THE NINTH CENTURY:** the folding knife has an overall length of 25 centimeters; the bronze blade is 10.5 centimeters long. The handle is made of bone; the handle butt depicts a stylized animal head, possibly a bird's head.

▸ **SWISS ARMY KNIFE OF THE ROMAN ERA:** this multi-part folding knife, dated to the third century, is made of silver and is provided with an iron blade, a spoon, a fork with three prongs, a toothpick, a tiny spatula, and a thorn.

From Sheffield to Around the Globe

Sheffield's fame was once based on two industrial branches: cutlery and steel. The production of steel already took a giant upsurge during the industrial revolution; the cutlery tradition goes back much further. On a tax list from 1297, a knife smith was mentioned for the first time: Robertus le Cotelar—Robert the Cutler. In the fourteenth century, knives from Sheffield were already so famous that they were mentioned in Geoffrey Chaucer's collection of stories *The Canterbury Tales*.

SHEFFIELD'S RISE
TO A CUTLERY METROPOLIS

Similar to Solingen, Sheffield is located in a region favored by nature. While in the Bergisches Land the river Wupper and its branches moved the old forging hammers and whetstones; in and around Sheffield no less than five rivers provided the needed force of water. Quickly, the city within the heart of England surpassed places such as Thaxted and Salisbury, which initially manufactured cutlery as well. Later, in the second half of the eighteenth century, even London's cutlery industry—still blooming in the beginning—had to declare itself defeated.

Even quite early, specialization was already taking place in Sheffield. The individual professional categories such as makers of scissors, scythes and sickles, file cutters, and knife smiths settled in different parts of the city and neighboring villages of Hallamshire. In 1624, by decree of the parliament the "Company of Cutlers in Hallamshire" was founded with Sheffield as its domicile. This guild organization kept the rights of the groups of craftsmen united in this guild, supervised the quality of the products, determined guidelines for the training, and regulated the registration of trademarks. At the top of this still-existing institution was the Master Cutler.

Around the mid seventeenth century three out of five male citizens of Sheffield worked in one of the branches of cutlery production. As in Solingen, the businesses were organized as "cottage industry": many small workshops, partly equipped with their own forges, were distributed around the city and its surroundings, each led by a master who usually was supported by a journeyman and an apprentice. The "little mesters"—that's how they called themselves—were able to work as free business people. Usually, the knowledge about the craft and the business was inherited from father to son.

During the nineteenth century besides the smaller units, larger manufactories were created, which employed several hundred workers. Partly the job positions in the factories were also rented to small businessmen. There was a close interlocking between factories and homeworkers and in the process the "little mesters" slipped more and more into dependency.

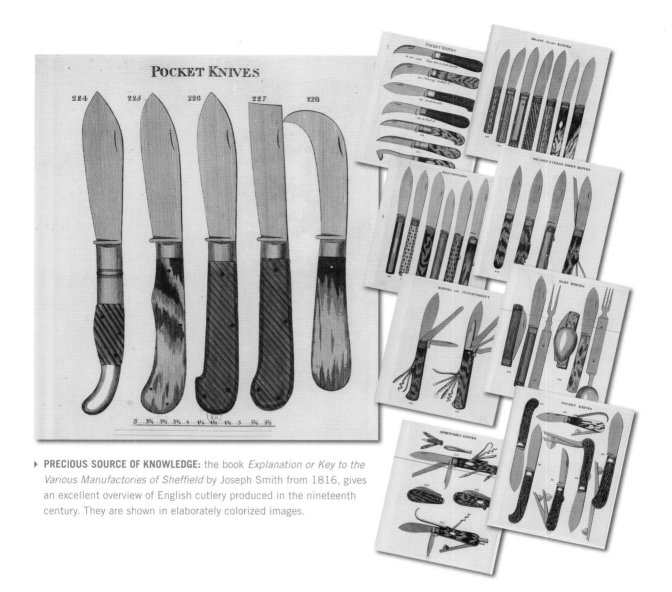

▶ **PRECIOUS SOURCE OF KNOWLEDGE:** the book *Explanation or Key to the Various Manufactories of Sheffield* by Joseph Smith from 1816, gives an excellent overview of English cutlery produced in the nineteenth century. They are shown in elaborately colorized images.

IMPORTANT INNOVATIONS

Sheffield's supremacy on the world market was based on groundbreaking innovations and on the commitment of enterprising entrepreneurs.

In the area of pocket knives, the back spring used since about the mid seventeenth century was a trend-setting innovation. The knives termed "spring knives"—commonly called slipjoints nowadays—have the unerring advantage over springless folders that the blade is kept in working position by the spring's tension. This technical innovation spread rapidly but was reserved for high-quality pocket knives. For the poor rural population the knife smiths in Sheffield for a long time kept producing the so-called "penny knives," simple and rustically constructed friction folders sold at a low price.

In the eighteenth century, a watch maker revolutionized the production and quality of blade steel from Sheffield. Benjamin Huntsman, born in 1704, was born into a German family that had emigrated to England only shortly prior to his birth. He learned the craft of a watchmaker and settled in Doncaster. Because he wasn't satisfied with the steel types available at that time, he experimented with various processes of steel production. After countless tries he finally succeeded in producing suitable cast steel in reusable crucibles. The heated, fluid steel could be cast into different shapes at will.

Although Huntsman initially was only thinking of better watch springs, he quickly realized the usefulness of his invention for all types of blades. Thus he moved into the vicinity of Sheffield, but initially couldn't convince the cutlery makers to adopt his innovation, because the cast steel was harder than the steel commonly used. Huntsman sold his products to France. Only when French cutlery made of Huntsman's cast steel conquered the English market did Sheffield's manufacturers feel compelled to use the new steel as well.

Huntsman gave up his watchmaking craft in 1751, and built a factory for the production of cast steel in Attercliffe—now a suburb of Sheffield. He managed the factory until his death in 1776. His former residence, which now houses a pub, has the year "1772" under its gable, whose ciphers, it is said, are made of cast steel. In hindsight,

Huntsman's innovation is the most important one in the history of Sheffield's industry.

The success of the cutlery made in Sheffield is to a considerable extent based on the special surface treatment. No other blade in the world has this velvet-like, anthracite-colored mirror shine the Sheffield blades had starting at about 1760. In Germany, Daniel Peres puzzled for about eight years trying to figure out the secret of the so-called "English polish."

But legend has it that the process was invented more or less without purpose. Apparently, Sheffield's scissor maker Robert Hinchliffe—who by the way was one of the first scissor makers to produce scissors of cast steel—wanted to delight his bride with an especially pretty example. During polishing he is supposed to inadvertently have reached for iron oxide powder (polishing red) instead of the usual polish. Regardless of how the polishing treatment was invented, it quickly spread throughout Sheffield and enormously increased the sales of the cutlery refined in that way.

TWO SUCCESS STORIES: JOSEPH RODGERS AND GEORGE WOSTENHOLM

Many well-known companies established Sheffield's great cutlery tradition. But in the nineteenth century there were especially two companies that fought with each other over the international leadership on the market: Joseph Rodgers & Sons and George Wostenholm. Besides Europe, they also conquered the markets of America, Africa, and Asia.

The world-famous trademark of the company Joseph Rodgers & Sons—a star and a Maltese cross—was first issued in 1682, but initially to some William Birks. In 1724, it went over to John Rodgers, and in 1764, was confirmed officially once more by the "Company of Cutlers." The company was named after Joseph Rodgers, who was born in 1743, and had four sons who all continued to lead the company after their father's death in 1821. In the same year the company was assigned by King George IV to be purveyor to the court. This assignment was renewed by the four following monarchs, which caused Joseph Rodgers to advertise with the self-confident slogan "the knife of kings, and the king of knives."

▶ **STAR AND MALTESE CROSS:** the famous brand sign of Joseph Rodgers & Sons was bound to no language and was recognized all over the world.

Initially, the family business produced exclusively pocket knives. Later, the assortment was extended

▶ **THE REPRESENTATIVE COMPANY'S SITE OF JOSEPH RODGERS & SONS:** in this building at Norfolk Street 6 several hundred workers were doing their job.

▶ **TEMPLE OF LUXURY:** the exclusive show and sales rooms of Joseph Rodgers & Sons presented cutlery like precious jewelry.

to include razors and table knives as well as scissors. In the Victorian era Joseph Rodgers rose to be the largest manufacturer of cutlery in the world. The showroom opened in Norfolk Street in 1822, and was a sensational novelty. In the 1860s, the exhibition and sales rooms were converted into pompous temples of luxury. In a dignified ambience the cutlery was presented in splendid display cabinets.

In 1840, Joseph Rodgers employed 520 staff members. Around the middle of the nineteenth century the name was so famous that Herman Melville, in his novel *Moby Dick* (1851), could naturally refer to "Roger's best cutlery" (the wrong spelling was probably unintentional by Melville). The Norfolk Knife, a display piece which was made over a period of two years for the World Expo in London in 1851, is still proof of the craftsmanship. The oversized pocket knife with its seventy-five-piece ensemble of blades and small tools is today on display in the Cutler's Hall in Sheffield.

The company Joseph Rodgers expanded to 1,200 employees in 1870, and had subsidiaries and store houses in London, New York, Montreal, Toronto, Havana, Bombay, and Calcutta. In the first decade of the twentieth century an estimated 1.6 million pocket knives left the factory each year—besides an equally impressive number of other cutlery wares.

The only competitor pushing into similar dimensions of business and succeeding, especially on the US market, was George Wostenholm.

Wostenholm, born in 1717, learned his craft from a knifesmith in Stannington and later established himself as "little mester." His great grandchild also had George as his first name and led the business to the top of the world. This George Wostenholm (1800–1876) was the one, who in 1831, was awarded the trademark I*XL, which had already been registered to another knifesmith in 1787. The word-play shortcut stands for "I excel" which could also be read as "I am excellent" or "I surpass everything."

Wostenholm had an ingenious talent for sales and was feared for his autocratic management style. He is said to have crossed the Atlantic thirty times during his lifetime to promote his business in the United States. As an expression of his close business relations with America, he named the factory building in Wellington Street, which he had bought in 1848, "Wellington Works." In 1855, 650 men, women, and children worked there. The production focused on high-quality pocket knives, hunting knives, and razors.

Wostenholm received the highest personal recognition when he became Master Cutler in 1856. Since his three marriages stayed childless, he sold the business one year prior to his death.

The crisis of Sheffield's cutlery industry did not pass Joseph Rodgers and George Wostenholm without leaving traces, but at least both companies were able to keep their businesses running until after World War II. But the production capacities and the assortments had to be adapted to the

▶ **THE NORFOLK KNIFE:** Joseph Rodgers made this imposing showpiece equipped with seventy-five blades and tools in two years of work. It is named after the company's office at Norfolk Street 6. It was presented to the public for the first time during the World Expo 1851, in London. Today it is on display in the Cutler's Hall in Sheffield.

drastically reduced demand. In 1971, the company Joseph Rodgers took over its formerly fiercest competitor, George Wostenholm. The new company, Rodgers Wostenholm, subsequently was sold several times and merged with other companies until it was finally liquidated in 1986.

THE END OF THE GLORY ERA

The downfall of the English cutlery industry started early when compared to Germany. Due to the restrictive protection policy of the United States, at the end of the nineteenth century the important American market collapsed for the English knife manufacturers. This loss could still be compensated by the sales markets in the British colonies. But at the same time the prices came under more and more pressure because the German manufacturers could produce cheaper than the technically more undeveloped workshops on the island. Finally, World War I sealed the fate of the English cutlery metropolis: workers of the factories in Sheffield died by the thousands on the battlefields of Europe.

In Sheffield, not much is left of the glorious fame of pocket knife production. Three of the most resounding names of former times—Joseph Rodgers, George Wostenholm, and George Ibberson—only exist as more or less faded brand names, which belong to Eggington Group since the mid 1980s. The company tries honestly to maintain the heritage and to continue the tradition by producing a manageable pallet of knives under the time-honored names. The models tie in with the classic patterns, among them pocket knives

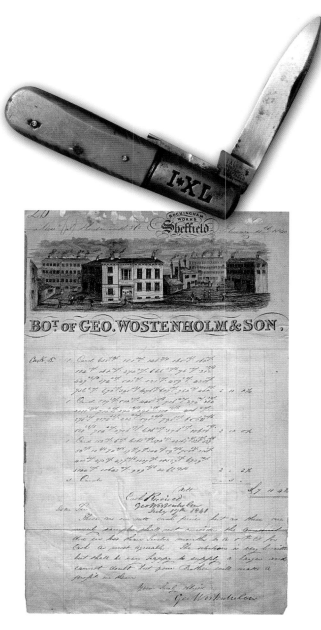

▶ **POCKET KNIFE AND AN OLD BILL OF GEORGE WOSTENHOLM:** the pocket knives with the famous I*XL logo were mostly exported to the United States.

with one or two parts, with spear point and sheepsfoot blades, as well as Barlow and garden knives. Even a very successful export article of the nineteenth century is represented: the Bowie knife.

The company Taylor's Eye Witness appears like a relic of former times. Despite many changes of ownership and names, it can look at a continuous history back to its year of foundation in 1838. Around 1890, the climax of its business success, several hundred people were on the company's payroll. Today, Taylor's Eye Witness is far from this, but in the historic manufactory building in Milton Street fine pocket knives are still produced in manual work.

The "little mesters," too, haven't vanished completely. A few independent knifemakers of Sheffield see their work as a continuation of the century-old tradition of craftsmanship which once founded the fame of the city.

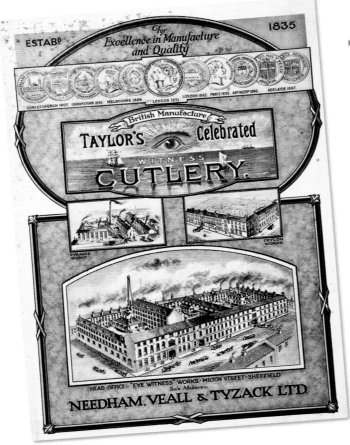

▶ OLD CATALOG PAGE OF NEEDHAM, VEALL & TYZACK: the brand name Taylor's Eye Witness outlived the company's name.

Solingen Is Catching Up

Solingen's legendary fame as blade city for centuries was based on the quality of the sword blades which were produced there since pre-medieval times. With the appearance of firearms the demand for edged weapons sank and many swordsmiths changed to cutlery, all the more since during the general refinement of table manners during the fifteenth and sixteenth centuries table knives became more and more fashionable.

But Solingen lagged behind for a long time with respect to another trend: while Sheffield produced elegant pen knives and pocket knives since the mid-seventeenth century, in Germany this industrial branch was not established until the nineteenth century.

FROM THE SYSTEM OF PRIVILEGES TO THE FREEDOM OF TRADE

The production of swords had matured over centuries to a process of distributed work which had created several specialized jobs. By and by these received the privilege of guilds: hardeners and grinders were first in 1401, in 1421, the sword polishers were allowed to form a guild, in 1472, the swordsmiths followed. Later (in 1571) the knifesmiths and the scissor makers (1793) founded their own guilds. The members of a guild were called "privileged." Whoever didn't belong to them was unprivileged and had to struggle hard.

The meticulous guild rules, the determination of wages and prices, as well as the limitation of rights and duties of the different guilds regularly led to conflicts. For example, there was a law suit lasting forty-five years dealing with the question whether a specific method of refinement should be done by the grinder or sword polisher. In addition, obsolete regulations were more and more in contradiction to the advancing technological development.

At the beginning of the nineteenth century, the archaic system of privileges paralyzed any innovation. When the Bergisches Land came under French administration in 1806, the end of the guild system was near. In 1809, Napoleon dissolved the guilds—from this time on every craftsman was able to do business freely. But the freedom of trade suddenly also increased the economic risk of the craftsmen, who—without the protection of the guilds –were now at the mercy of the free play of market forces.

AHEAD OF TIME: DANIEL PERES

Into this time of changes came the efforts of a man who attempted to lift the cutlery of Solingen onto the level of the products from Sheffield. The merchant Daniel Peres, born in Solingen in 1776, had come to know the superior quality of English products during his travels through the Netherlands. He was impressed by the "English polish" and knew that this unique feature was decisive for the monopolistic dominance of Sheffield's cutlery. With tireless endurance he managed to unravel the chemical composition of the polishing means after eight years of trying.

But as an unprivileged merchant Peres had to proceed with tact in order to commercially exploit his "re-invention." Thus in 1801, he submitted a request to the government in Düsseldorf, in which he asked for the right to build a factory. Despite the fierce opposition of the guilds, the state government gave him the concession. In the same year, already the corner stone for the building, named "Birmingham," by Peres was set. (Why it wasn't called "Sheffield" is a question passionately discussed in circles of local historians.)

Peres was forward-looking in all respects: he was the first to relocate the water wheel, usually mounted on the outside, into the center of the building to allow continuous work even in winter.

▶ **DANIEL PERES (1776–1845):** the merchant from Solingen was a pioneer of cutlery production.

The production, which started in 1803, first focused on different kinds of scissors. In 1805, Peres received permission to also produce pen knives, pocket knives, and razors. On the one hand, this way he avoided the privileged, because nobody had produced this kind of wares in Solingen before he did. On the other hand, he pushed into just the market segment dominated by Sheffield.

The biggest problem for Peres was to keep his polishing secret. He obligated his employees to discretion under oath—but without success. Around 1804, the polishing method was already common among the entire cutlery industry of Solingen. In addition, other manufacturers as well resorted to the production of pen- and pocket knives. Some competitors even tried to get Peres' trademark. And last but not least, the outer circumstances afflicted the young business: during the French foreign rule the Continental Blockade and rigid customs tariffs impeded the import of raw materials and the export of wares. After the end of the "French period," as it was called then, Daniel Peres continued to manage the factory for another couple of years, but in 1823, felt forced to stop production. Thereafter he and his son dedicated themselves to trade with cutlery from Solingen. Only in 1878, did his grandchildren start new production.

Daniel Peres was an untimely pioneer who had to fight against the resistance of an outdated economic system. But he deserves lasting credit for pushing technical innovations, this way strengthening Solingen's competitiveness towards Sheffield.

FROM WORKSHOPS WITH WATER WHEELS TO POLISHING WITH STEAM ENGINES

You should not imagine the factory of Daniel Peres as a giant hall with hundreds of workers. The building was just a large workshop with a water wheel and a dam with accompanying pond and did not differ much from the other about 120 workshops along the river Wupper and the creeks in the Bergisches Land.

Up to the twentieth century these polishing workshops were integrated in a decentralized production process. The small workshops were in the possession of one or several families and were also used as housing space. The number of polishing positions varied with the size of the building; partly the workplaces were also rented to independent grinders. The other job groups as well, such as hardeners, the people mounting the parts of the knives, cleaning and polishing them, and the ones making the handle shields, did their jobs in homework.

The manufacturers, in turn, were merchants who themselves neither had machines nor tools but brought in their capital. They bought the raw materials of the smiths and organized the further

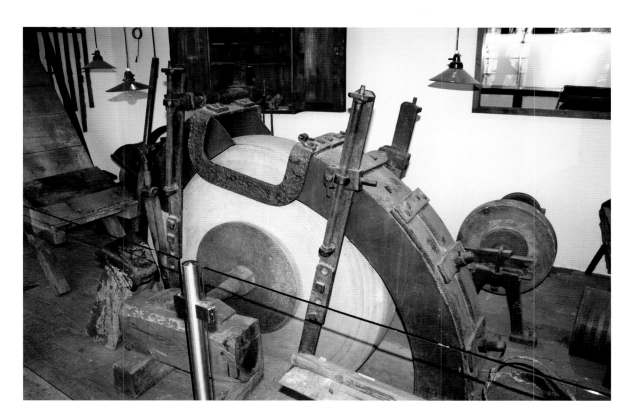

▶ **GLANCE INTO A GRINDING WORKSHOP (SCHLEIFERMUSEUM BALKHAUSER KOTTEN):** this was what the workplace of a grinder looked like in the nineteenth century.

refinement by hardeners, grinders, and the people mounting the parts and polishing the knives until they were able to sell the finished products in the end.

The transport of wares between smiths, grinding workshops, and the offices of the producers was usually done by the wives of the grinders. These so-called "delivery women"—*Liewerfrauen*" in the dialect of Solingen—shaped the image of the landscape and city up to the twentieth century. The women carried the wares in large baskets on their heads and had to walk on the exhausting paths through the valley of the Wupper in all kinds of weather. Similar to the "buffer girls" in Sheffield, who polished the metal wares, the delivery women

had an important function in the organization of work within Solingen's cutlery industry.

As the force of water was replaced by the steam engine and later on by the electric motor, the grinders left their "*Wasserkotten*" (workshops with water wheels) and moved to the vicinity of the industrial factories. The delivery women were no longer needed. By the end of the 1950s, they were honored by the city of Solingen with a bronze sculpture as a memorial.

The use of steam force was only slowly established in the Bergisches Land because water force was abundantly available and, in addition, was free of charge. The steam engine technology primarily revolutionized the forging process. In combination with the new technique of die-forging it was possible to produce raw wares in great variety and high quantity. In the vicinity of the die-forges the first large steam grinderies were built, some of which were large enough for more than 200 grinders. Most grinding positions were rented to independent grinders.

At the beginning of the twentieth century, when Solingen was region-wide provided with electrical energy, the steam-driven grinderies by and by lost their influence. While at their peak in 1897, 107 steam-driven grinderies existed, only six remained in 1913. Though some companies converted to electric drives, many grinders established motor workshops of their own.

▸ **DELIVERY WOMEN OF SOLINGEN AROUND 1934:** the wives of the grinders transported the goods between the workshops.

INDUSTRIAL PRODUCTION
AND HOMEWORK

An article published in 1853, comparing the production types in Solingen and Sheffield states about Solingen: "Manufactories in the sense in which the product is manufactured from beginning to finish, the like of which can be found in Sheffield, don't exist here." This state changed during the last third of the nineteenth century, when the first larger factory complexes were built, whose imposing brick facades and smoking chimneys from then on decorated the heads of letters and bills (the graphic designers in these cases didn't especially care about the real ratio of sizes).

The steel and cutlery company Gottlieb Hammesfahr, whose origin dates back to the year 1684, was one of the largest industrial businesses in Solingen up to the twentieth century. There, not only knives, scissors, and flatware of all kinds were manufactured and sold under the famous trademarks Pyramide and Nirosta, but in addition the drop-forge owned by the company delivered raw wares to other manufacturers. Another industrial giant, the company Zwilling J.A. Henckels, in the 1920s, employed 2,500 staff members; 1,200 of them in the factory, 1,300 as homeworkers. Friedrich Herder Abraham in its best times, in comparison, had a moderate 450 employees at the company and equally as many homeworkers. These numbers mirror the distribution of work in the entire industrial sector: around 1925, about half of the workers in the cutlery industry were homeworkers.

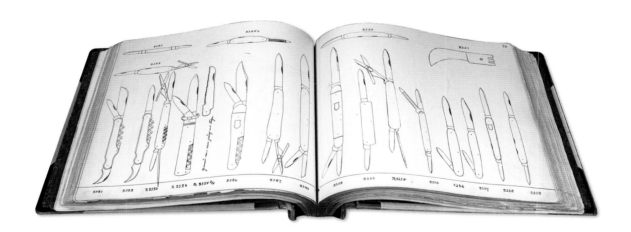

▸ **MODEL BOOK OF THE COMPANY ROBERT KLAAS (OF THE 1930S):** every available model is depicted as a detailed ink drawing.

The traditional commercial work at home with its demanding manual work sustained its position over a long period as a complement to the mechanized production processes within the factories. But after World War II, homework was in steady decline. On the one hand, more and more machines were used in the newly erected factories, on the other hand, in many classic homework businesses young talents were missing.

THE DEVELOPMENT OF SOLINGEN'S POCKET KNIFE PRODUCTION

Although at the beginning of the nineteenth century Solingen was far behind Sheffield in the area of fine pocket knives, the tides turned towards the end of the century. The competitive advantages of before—cast steel and steel polish—played no role anymore. For a long time already, cast steel had no longer been imported from England, but from the Ruhr district, and the businesses at Solingen at that time were also proficient in surface refinement.

In the second half of the nineteenth century, about fifty years after Daniel Peres' failed attempt to establish a pocket knife manufactory, a founding wave of pocket knife manufactories emerged. Some companies of Solingen managed to gain a foothold in the US market with high-quality products and to wrest market shares from Sheffield's competitors. Because of the knifesmiths and grinders who had emigrated from the Bergisches Land, family relationships already existed with the New World.

In the middle of the nineteenth century, the manufactory Robert Klaas established business contacts within the United States. The company Heinr. Böker & Co., which was founded in 1869, exported the majority of its products to America around 1900. Later a branch of the family Böker even established a manufactory of its own in New York. A multitude of other companies as well had subsidiaries and store houses in foreign countries. The figurehead of the exported cutlery goods was always pocket knives, because they were the most obvious proof of craftsmanship.

To overcome the language barrier on the English-speaking markets, companies from Solingen named themselves with English expressions or registered English brand names. Robert Hartkopf, for example, called his enterprise "Hudson Cutlery Works," and brands such as "Uncle Sam" (Robert Klaas) or "Daniel Boone" (Gebrüder Krusius) distinctly targeted the US market. Strong figurative trademarks such as Carl Schliepers' "Eye Brand" or Böker's "Tree Brand" also asserted themselves in many other countries.

An almost unbelievable variety of pocket knives, from present-day perspective, was manufactured in Solingen from the end of the nineteenth century up to the First World War, which is verified by the pattern books and catalogs of this time. In a forty-eight page 1904 catalog from the Wüsthof company, 1,125 different pocket knife models are pictured! Although the First World War cut off Solingen from its most important export markets, leading to a shrinking of production, the pattern variety of the pocket knives produced in the 1920s was still immense.

During World War II, some cutlery manufactories were heavily damaged, their pattern books and records were lost, machines and tools destroyed. The companies which still had a halfway-intact infrastructure after the war ended, soon were at a disadvantage compared to the companies which were erected anew and furnished with modern machines.

The years of the "*Wirtschaftswunder*" ("economic miracle," the booming years of the 1950s and early 1960s) were able to hide for a while that the pocket knives from Solingen were on the retreat compared to other cutlery. As a first measure, the assortments were rigorously cut down. As the demand continuously sank in the mid-1960s, and the costs for labor rose, more and more pocket knife manufactories—especially small companies—had to give up their business. The victorious advance of the Swiss Army Knife also added to their downfall. Big companies, such as Wüsthof and Zwilling, closed down their pocket knife divisions. And finally the cheap competitors from overseas added their weight to push Solingen's pocket knives from the market.

And today? The few cutlery companies of Solingen which still have a pocket knife production of their own follow different approaches. The company Böker, for example, successfully placed their emphasis on a combination of the premium pocket knives produced in Solingen with knives produced abroad, which are marketed under the brand names "Böker Plus" and "Magnum by Böker." The extensive palette of models distinguishes itself by modern designs which are partly created by cooperating with internationally renowned knifemakers. But traditional patterns are also regularly part of the assortment.

Puma, one of the oldest cutlery companies of Solingen, also offers a mixture of in-house production and imported wares with the focus on hunting and outdoors. This also holds in a similar way for the palette of Linder's products. Other manufacturers occupy special niches: Hubertus, for example, has an extraordinarily large collection of traditional pocket hunting knives, the company Otter is especially well-known for their Mercator knife, and the cutlery company Lütters, founded in 1840, and—believe it or not—producing 20,000 different models during the 1920s, now specializes in professional knives for fishery, agriculture, and other kinds of industry.

The manufactories of Solingen most closely associated with classic, handmade gentleman's pocket knives nowadays are Friedrich Hartkopf, Robert Klaas, and Friedrich Olbertz, the latter mainly producing for the American market. Whether these pocket knives have any future depends on two factors: the demand and trainees.

America's Golden Age

The United States was the most important market outlet for Sheffield's cutlery up to the end of the nineteenth century. The local village smiths provided the American rural population with axes, scythes, sickles, and other tools. But with respect to fine razor blades, pen- or pocket knives, the products of the former motherland were without competition.

An early export hit from Sheffield was the Barlow knife, which later turned into a genuine American icon. People in Britain always had a keen sense for the market trends on the other side of the Atlantic. When the Bowie knife—another American legend—became fashionable towards the end of the 1820s, the manufacturers in Sheffield reacted quickly and started mass production of the coveted knife, which was exported to the United States in enormous numbers during the following decades. English producers set new trends with clever marketing chess moves: the pocket knife patterns with the exclusive-sounding names "Senator" and "Congress" were most probably developed in Sheffield and targeted especially for the US market.

When the United States government drastically raised the duties on foreign steel wares by means of the McKinley Tariff Act of 1890, the dominance of English imports was broken. The driving force behind this protectionist policy was the lobby of the American cutlery industry, which in the meantime had been growing into an important economic factor. During the following years the US government continued its protectionism with new and ever-changing laws.

The effect was sweeping: the pure trading companies which imported cutlery from England and Germany into the United States lost their business models almost overnight. The native pocket knife producers in turn lived through an unparalleled upsurge around the turn of the century. The period between 1890 and the early 1940s, is often called America's Golden Age of Pocket Knives. Some collectors even claim that no pocket knives of matching quality have ever been made since then.

IMMIGRANTS FROM SHEFFIELD AS FOUNDERS OF START-UPS

The first knife manufactories built on American soil during the nineteenth century were mostly founded by knifesmiths emigrated from England, who brought the know-how they had collected in Sheffield over to the New World. There they hoped for better possibilities to unfold their talents. Compared to the many German emigrants from the Bergisches Land, they had the advantage of being proficient in the language. Many of them settled in Connecticut. Two of these immigrants who fundamentally influenced America's pocket knife industry were Samuel Mason and Charles W. Platts.

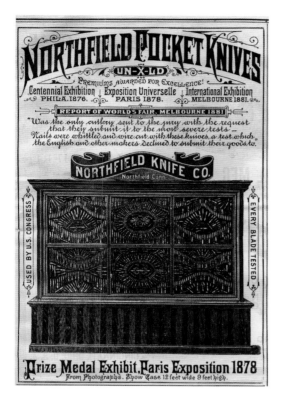

▸ **HISTORIC PREMIUM BRAND:** the Northfield Knife Company set standards in the American knife industry with its brand UN-X-LD, introduced in 1876.

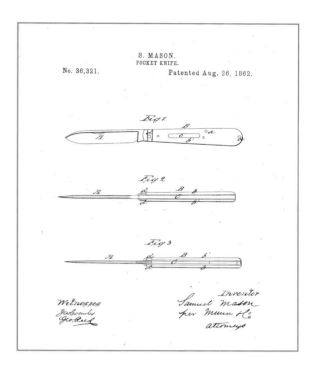

▸ **PATENT DRAWING BY SAMUEL MASON:** the patent with the number 36.321 of August 26, 1862, describes the construction of a pocket knife with handle scales of malleable cast iron which show an outside structure similar to stag and also imitate the conventional bolsters.

When the skilled "master cutler" Samuel Mason, who had learned his craftsmanship in the renowned Sheffield company Joseph Mappin & Sons, came to the United States in 1840, he had already accumulated twenty years of professional experience. Within the United States he was prominent in setting up the Northfield Knife Company, founded in 1858. Mason developed several patents for enhancing pocket knives and later on participated in several other cutlery start-ups. At age fifty-five he returned to England.

In 1864, the young and talented Charles W. Platts left Sheffield, where he had been trained at Joseph Rodgers & Sons among other companies. Eight years later he got the job as production manager at Northfield, a post he kept for more than twenty years. Under his aegis the brand UN-X-LD was introduced in 1876, which set a new quality standard for pocket knives made in the United States. The knives of this brand repeatedly received awards at international exhibitions.

Charles W. Platts had five sons, who all found employment in the cutlery industry. After an intermezzo at Cattaragus Cutlery he, together with his sons, in 1896, founded the C. Platts & Sons Cutlery Company in Gowanda, New York. There the Platts produced pocket knives especially for the Case Brothers. Shortly thereafter, when the rooms became too small, the family business moved to Eldred, Pennsylvania. The factory building in Gowanda was sold in 1897, to a young and aspiring company which, too, soon became noteworthy: Schatt & Morgan.

DYNAMIC AND DYNASTIES

The history of American pocket knife manufactories was shaped by an enormous dynamic. In the second half of the nineteenth century, especially after the end of the American Civil War, many companies were founded that vanished after a short period of time or were taken over by competitors. The new owner usually added the acquired raw materials and semifinished goods to his own production, with the effect that pocket knives were offered on the market by company A, with the name of perished company B still marked on the blade.

▸ **WITNESSES OF THE GOLDEN AGE:** these five back lock folders originate from the era of Schatt & Morgan.

From time to time manufactories were renamed or changed the trademarks on their blades. This became regularly the case. Quite often knives made in the United States were masqueraded as being English or German products. And when the spirit of the time required patriotic attitude, it could be of advantage to sell imported cutlery under American labels. If you also take into account that many factories exclusively produced for outside companies, it becomes clear that a lot of detective work is still waiting for historians and collectors who want to unravel the threads of American pocket knife history.

▶ **JOHN RUSSELL "RUSS" CASE (1878–1953):** this self-made man led the fortunes of W.R. Case & Sons for more than fifty years.

Over time, family dynasties formed, whose members quite often were involved in several businesses at once. And as soon as one family had established itself successfully, individual members cut loose and established businesses on their own. The most famous example is John Russell "Russ" Case who at first worked as a traveling salesman for Case Brothers, the company of his three uncles. When his relatives saw that Russ earned more money with his commissions than they themselves did, they wanted to cut his salary. Quickly Russ turned his back on his uncles and in 1902, with the help of his father William Russell—the person behind the initials "W.R."—founded his own company, the W.R. Case & Sons Cutlery Company.

In addition, the influential families of the cutlery industry strived hard to strengthen their market power by means of skillful marriage policy. But maybe it was true love which in 1892, led to the marriage of Harvey N. Platts, the oldest son of Charles W. Platts, and Debbie Case. In 1905, the families Platts and Case also banded together more closely commercially and together set up a new factory in Bradford, Pennsylvania. They christened the new company W.R. Case & Sons Cutlery Company. Note the added plural "s" which was definitely justified because Harvey N. Platts was the son-in-law of W.R. Case. Both managers related by marriage complemented one another in an optimal way: the sales talent of Russ provided for a constant flow of orders while Harvey, with his know-how in technical production, took care of the manufactory's flawless operation.

LOGO SWINDLE

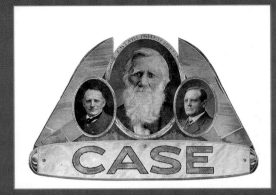

The first logo of W.R. Case & Sons quite often is jokingly called "Father, Son, and Holy Job," because it shows three generations: at the right, company founder Russ Case; at left father, W.R. Case; and in the center, grandfather Job Case (who, by the way, did not make a single knife during his entire life). Remarkable is the year on top of Job's portrait: "Established 1847!" Clever marketing strategist Russ Case gave his business, which was founded in 1902, from scratch a fifty-five-year old history by simply declaring his father's year of birth to be the founding year of his company. The patriarchal three-generation image and the date provided the company with an aura of reputation and tradition.

POCKET KNIFE PRODUCTION UNDER A SINGLE ROOF

Around the turn of the century, American pocket knife manufactories were geographically concentrated in two states: the Case Brothers and, up to 1905, W.R. Case & Sons as well, were located in Little Valley, New York—as were Cattaraugus Cutlery (1886–1903) and Brown Brothers (1890–1902), to name just a few well-known companies. In nearby Gowanda, Schatt & Morgan produced since 1897. About one hundred kilometers southwest of Little Valley a lot of companies had settled down in Pennsylvania; in Tidioute alone five manufactories existed at one time. Later, the region around Tidioute and Bradford was called "the Magic Circle of Cutlery."

While in Solingen the production of pocket knives was distributed over the entire city, pocket knives in American factories were usually made there from A to Z. The factory of Schatt & Morgan, for example, around 1900, was divided into six departments. In the "Material Department" forty mechanics and smiths were working on making the forging dies, forging blades, and punching out bolsters, liners, and springs. The machines were driven by a 50 hp electric motor. In the "Tempering Department" there was a—for those times—state-of-the-art gas-heated heat treatment facility for hardening blades and springs. The "Grinding Department" was the workplace of the grinders, and in the "Assembly Department" the pocket knives were put together. In the "Handle Finishing Department" and "Blade Finishing Department" the fine treatment of handles and

▶ **GROUP PHOTO IN FRONT OF THE FACTORY BUILDING OF SCHATT & MORGAN IN TITUSVILLE, PENNSYLVANIA (1914):** the two businessmen, John W. Schatt and Charles B. Morgan, created one of the most renowned pocket knife brands of the early twentieth century.

▶ **A VIEW OF THE FACTORY OF QUEEN CITY CUTLERY (1922):** the pocket knife manufactory was founded in 1922, by five former employees of Schatt & Morgan and still exists today (but without the word "City" in the name).

blades was done. The factory was set up for a daily production volume of 3,500 pocket knives.

The factories of other companies were organized in a similar way. The forging divisions were a constant source of danger because open fires were used there. Factory fires at that time were a quite common phenomenon anyway and thus it is no wonder that both founders of Schatt & Morgan launched a private fire department in Gowanda, the C.B. Morgan Hose Company. The Case Brothers had to experience how devastating a factory fire can be. In February 1912, the factory in Little Valley burnt down to its foundations. The company was unable to recover from this setback. A new factory was erected, but because of their high debts, the uncles of Russ Case had to shut down the company in 1915.

A GERMAN CLIMBS THE CAREER LADDER: ADOLPH KASTOR

In the twentieth century true cutlery giants such as Imperial or Camillus were created in the United States. One number to emphasize this fact: in 1940, Imperial produced more than 100,000 knives daily! But like the great names from Sheffield, the American industrial giants from the past are now only present with their trademarks, mostly decorating cheap imported wares from China distributed elsewhere.

It was a German from the Palatine who at the beginning of the twentieth century laid the foundation for the cutlery empire Camillus which closed down in 2007. Adolph Kastor came to New York as a fourteen-year old boy in 1870, and literally worked his way from the bottom to the top in the hardware store of his uncle: from the cow chains in the cellar to the knives on the topmost floor. Six years later he founded his own company, which specialized in trading with cutlery imported from England and Germany.

Adolph Kastor and his younger brothers constructed a widely branching trade network from their office in New York. Nathan, the older brother, dealt with buying the wares in Solingen. But during the 1890s, the rigid protectionism of the US government deprived the company of its basis for business, thus forcing Kastor to look for inland production possibilities. He found them in the small town Camillus in the state of New York. In 1894, Charles E. Sherwood had founded a manufactory there, producing a small assortment of pocket knives with the help of twenty workers— many of them from Sheffield. Kastor the businessman realized the potential of the small manufactory and bought it in 1902. This was the hour of birth for Camillus Cutlery Company.

Kastor invested in new machines and introduced an efficient division of labor. He didn't have to wait long for success. In 1910, Camillus already had about 200 employees, and almost a million knives left the factory per year. Kastor appreciated the sense for quality in his former fellow countrymen and purposefully hired qualified workers from Germany, for whom he even built separate living quarters ("Germania Hall").

During the First World War Camillus to a large extent produced knives, marlinspikes, and scalpels for the American forces. But the many Germans

▸ **ADOLPH KASTOR (1856–1946):** came from Germany as a fourteen-year-old immigrant to the United States and later established the cutlery empire Camillus.

▸ **PROUD CAMILLUS WORKERS ABOUT 1909:** Adolph Kastor purposefully hired German fellow countrymen, whose qualities he appreciated.

raised the distrust of the US authorities. It is said that even a spy was planted in the factory to uncover possible plans for sabotage. But fears that the German workers might blow up the factory proved to be unfounded.

In 1927, Adolph Kastor retreated from active business and handed the company over to his son Alfred. During the 1920s and 1930s, Camillus broadened its pallete of models and steadily raised its production capacities. Commissioned production developed into an extremely profitable business: almost all the knives in the catalogs of large household goods and hardware dealers came from the Camillus factory.

During World War II Camillus once again received huge orders from the US military. The almost 700 employees worked in shifts all around the clock. An estimated fifteen million knives were delivered to the armed forces between 1942–1945—from knives for electricians, foldable machetes for pilots, up to various combat knives. After the war Camillus continued to push its expansion. Companies were bought, new brands established. The Vietnam War once again brought military orders to Camillus.

But a few decades later decreasing demand, management errors, and the cheap competition from Asia sealed the downfall of the long-established

American company with German roots. In 2007, Camillus had to declare bankruptcy—not a glamorous ending; Imperial Schrade had ended the same way three years earlier.

POCKET KNIVES FOR COLLECTORS

Today there are only a handful of manufacturers among the American knife producers who still make their pocket knives the traditional way. It is especially due to the collecting passion of many Americans that such pocket knives still exist. The historical interest in the classics of American pocket knife tradition and the collecting passion linked to it started in the 1960s. Soon thereafter the first collector's clubs were founded and the first pocket knife guides published. Today there is at least one collector's club in each of the states whose members meet regularly to talk shop about their latest acquisitions. Local knife shows where enthusiasts and dealers meet are also quite popular.

Dealers also seek active communication with collectors. W.R. Case & Sons, for example, in 1981, founded the Case Collectors Club, whose members receive a magazine and special offers. On a global scale the communicative exchange among collectors takes place in the internet. The platform iKnife Collector (www.iknifecollector.com) is a popular meeting point on the web with respect to traditional American pocket knives.

Besides market leader Case, which after several changes of ownership is now part of the Zippo corporate group, the manufactory Queen Cutlery—founded in 1922, by former employees of Schatt & Morgan in Titusville, Pennsylvania—was also able to survive in difficult times. Back in family ownership since 2012, Queen produces fine pocket knives mainly for the collector's market. The heritage of Imperial Schrade is also still alive in a special way. Although the rights to the trademarks Imperial Schrade, Old Timer, and Uncle Henry today are in possession of Taylor Brands, former employees of Imperial Schrade founded the manufactory Canal Street Cutlery in Ellenville, New York, where they produce small series of traditional pocket knives.

The potential of the collector's market is proven by the still fresh success story of the company Great Eastern Cutlery (GEC) that was founded in 2006, when almost nobody in the knife industry would have given even the slightest hint of a chance for a new producer of traditional pocket knives. The two founders are old players: Bill Howard had been chief designer at Queen Cutlery before, and Ken Daniels stems from a family working in the knife trade for generations.

GEC assured itself the rights to two legendary historical brands: Northfield UN-X-LD and Tidioute Cutlery. The company moved to the former factory building of Cyclops Steel in Titusville and started to produce pocket knives—in the same way as they were produced about one hundred years ago. The excellent quality of workmanship made the rounds and gave the manufactory a loyal basis of customers. Each month new mini series of traditional pocket knives are released which mirror the glamour of America's Golden Age.

▶ **GOLDEN AGE "RELOADED":** the company Great Eastern Cutlery, founded in 2006, has revived two great traditional brands—Tidioute Country and Northfield UN-X-LD.

CHAPTER 3

A BIT OF POCKET KNIFE SCIENCE

Anatomy of a Pocket Knife

The construction of a folding knife varies from model to model; nevertheless there are many common characteristics. Pocket knives made in the traditional way usually have a riveted construction which can't be taken apart. Many modern folders, in contrast, are screwed together, which has the advantage that the knife can be taken apart for cleaning. In addition, the play of the blade can be adjusted by means of the axis screw.

Apart from a few exceptions where the handle is milled from a single piece of wood, horn, or titanium, most pocket knife handles are made of two halves. If handle materials such as titanium, stainless steel, or other stable materials like G-10 are used, the handle scales themselves are the supporting structure. In all other cases stabilizing liners are used, which are usually made of brass. The liners are either a separate layer within the construction of the handle or are placed in corresponding depressions of the handle scales. To reduce weight, steel liners are often provided with drill holes and recesses.

A classic component of a traditional pocket knife is the bolsters, which are mounted in pairs at one or both handle ends. Usually they are made of nickel silver, stainless steel, or brass. The front bolsters give stability to the axis rivet; at the rear handle end they protect the handle scales from spalling. But often the bolsters have only a decorative function.

The examples of a traditional and a modern lockback folder reveal the similarities and differences of their construction.

TRADITIONAL LOCKBACK FOLDER

1 Blade
2 Liner
3 Pins for riveting
4 Bolsters
5 Handle scales
6 Locking lever
7 Spacer with spring

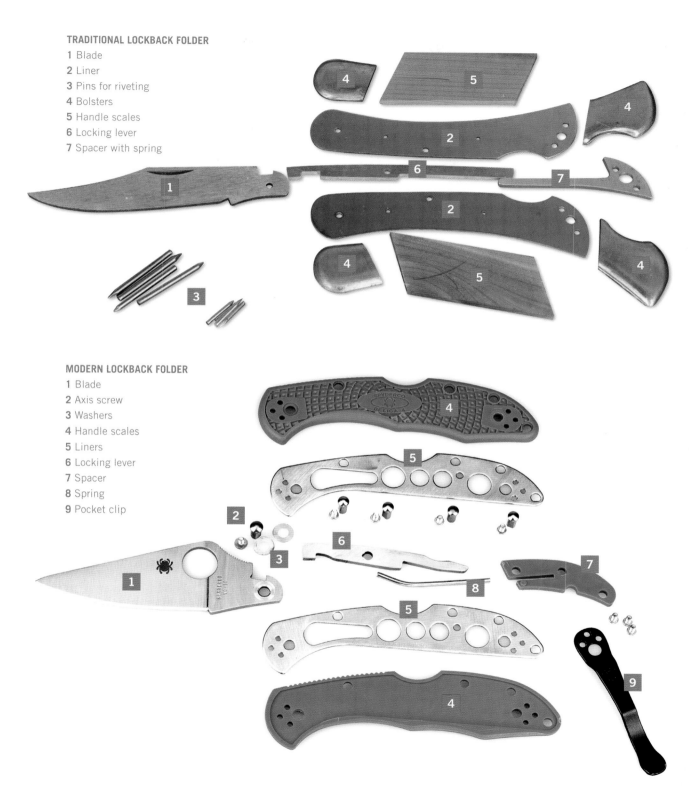

MODERN LOCKBACK FOLDER

1 Blade
2 Axis screw
3 Washers
4 Handle scales
5 Liners
6 Locking lever
7 Spacer
8 Spring
9 Pocket clip

Handle Materials

Basically every material that is strong and durable is suitable for making knife handles. Initially, natural products from the region were used: in the far north of Europe reindeer antlers and masur birch were plentiful; in Mediterranean areas olive wood as well as bones and horns of local farm animals were the obvious choice.

The handles of traditional pocket knives are still covered with wood, bones, cow, buffalo horn, or stag. The once popular mother-of-pearl is only rarely used today. Manufacturers of modern folders mostly use titanium, aluminum, or robust plastics and composite materials. In both areas you can also see a trend towards more and more exotic materials: Laguiole knives with handle scales from mammoth molars are as sought after as are modern-designed pocket knives with handles from meteorite iron. In general: there is nothing which isn't available.

WOOD

Wood has been a popular handle material since prehistoric times. Some knife enthusiasts value the pleasantly warm touch, others enjoy the expressive grain structure of certain woods. It is said that there are also people who regularly sniff their pocket knife with juniper wood handles because they love the pepper-like smell emitted by the wood.

The association of the landscape with the origin of the knife hardly plays a role today. Even a pocket knife with a patriotic name such as Le Français made by Perceval is available with handle scales of desert ironwood, although Olneya tesota, as it is called in botany, is only at home in Arizona, California, and parts of Mexico. Of course, there are exceptions: the turned handles of French Nontron knives have always been made from regional boxwood. And the owner of the manufactory JHP uses bog oak from the peat bogs of his homeland, the Grand Brière in Western France, not only for knife handles, and even digs out the up-to-5,000-year-old oak trunks himself.

Depending on the plant species, not only trunk and branches are used, but also the roots or knots created by anomalies in growth. Nowadays almost any type of wood is used for the production of handle scales. Wood types with large pore structure or low density are stabilized by a special process prior to use: the air is sucked from the cavities of the wood by means of a vacuum, then artificial resin of low viscosity is pressed into all pores and capillaries down to the smallest ones. In addition, the stabilizing resin can also be mixed with dye. After hardening, the wood is permanently stable and insensitive to moisture and temperature changes. This way even wood infested with fungi can be processed.

Knife manufacturers usually avail themselves of the wide assortment that specialized companies offer, such as Raffir, which stabilizes woods from all over the world and delivers them cut to block size or the size of scales. For enthusiasts and collectors pocket knives, whose woods have a story of their own, are especially interesting. For example, in 1999, a storm raged through the Versailles park and knocked over centuries-old trees. Guy Vitalis bought part of the wood and provided his sommelier and pocket knives with it.

BONE

In former times, humans all over the world made small things for use or decoration from animal bones and teeth. The sailors on the whaling ships of the eighteenth and nineteenth centuries passed their time carving artsy things (also knife handles) from the bones and teeth of sperm whales or from walrus tusks. The scrimshaw technique also stems from the time of the whalers: a scratching and engraving technique still decorating the handles of artistically made custom knives nowadays.

By means of the industrialization of meat production in the nineteenth century, huge amounts of bone became waste. The slaughterhouses at that time were happy that the knife factories took the animal remains. Because of their size and density, the shin bones of cattle were especially well suited for the production of pocket knife handle scales. Quite soon specialized companies existed for boiling, dyeing, and milling the bones. In the United States the two companies, Rogers and Winterbottom, became market leaders who, during the first half of the twentieth century,

▸ **STABILIZED AND DYED:** today, almost any wood type can be used to make handle scales.

▸ **BONE:** Case processes large amounts of this natural material every year.

▸ **STAG ANTLERS:** this material is traditionally used for hunting knives and gentleman's folders.

▸ **HORN:** regional pocket knives from Italy and France are often provided with horn handles.

provided practically the entire American pocket knife industry with prefabricated handle scales.

To enhance the grip of the material, patterns were milled into the surface ("jigged bone"). Experts can determine the origin of the scales by means of the milled patterns of this time: while Winterbottom-scales can be determined by means of their elongated, fluted depressions, Rogers milled a random pattern of small grooves into the bones and polished the raised parts flat. "Rogers Stag" in these times became a trademark for bone scales which were dyed and milled in such a way that they imitated the look of stag antlers. The expression "bone stag" is still used for stag-like handle scales made of bone, and the classic milling patterns of Rogers and Winterbottom are still copied today.

After 1945, most knife manufacturers focused on plastics as handle material for the future. Only the company Case consistently stayed with this well-proven natural product, even though it used other materials besides. Today Case processes a considerable amount of cattle bone per year, imported from South America. Dyeing and milling are done in their own factory. The new knives introduced each year differ from the ones of the previous season mainly by the dominating colors of the bone scales.

This wasn't always the case. Apart from exceptions, up to the 1990s, Case did not even give explicit names to the colors of the bone material. But today there are—similar to the world of fashion—recurring color classics such as "navy blue,"

"moss green," or "golden rod." Other manufacturers of traditional pocket knives, too, prefer to use bone in addition to wood.

HORN AND STAG

Handle scales of cow or buffalo horn can mainly be seen on regional pocket knives from France and Italy, where these natural products have a long tradition. The high-quality scales are cut from the robust tip of the horn. But only in rare cases does the horn really stem from regional animals. Indian zebus and water buffalos deliver the bulk of the horn processed in Europe. The pocket knives are usually offered with smoothly polished scales of bright or dark horn (in French called "corne blonde" and "corne noir"). Ram's horn is an interesting handle material, too, because its rustic surface structure provides each knife handle with a character of its own.

Stag is traditionally linked to hunting and thus it is no wonder that especially pocket knives for hunting are equipped with this material. But it is also a permanent fixture among other pocket knife types. While real stag nowadays is not exquisite but nevertheless belongs to upmarket materials, in the early nineteenth century even cheap mass products were provided with it. The outer husk of the antler is used as well as the leftover, inner material seen as being of inferior quality ("second cut"). Sometimes the stag is treated with a burner ("burnt stag") to achieve an amber-colored to dark-brown hue. For quality reasons stag is mainly imported from India:

because of their higher density, the antlers of the South Asian Sambar deer are superior to the more porous antlers of Western species.

If the expression "genuine stag" is used in the description of a pocket knife, this means that the stag in principle can be from any animal with antlers (e.g. moose).

FOSSILIZED MATERIALS

Within the framework of CITES (the Convention on International Trade in Endangered Species of Wild Fauna and Flora), international trade with ivory was prohibited in 1999. Within the European Union, only registered old stock with proof of origin is allowed to be processed. Therefore ivory is the most used by artistic knifemakers for special one-of-a-kind pieces. It has completely vanished from serial production.

Instead of this, fossil bones and teeth of extinct primeval animals are increasingly gaining in popularity. The bones, tusks, and molars of mammoths retrieved from the thawing permafrost of Northern Siberia serve as material for handle scales of high-end pocket knives. The natural grain as well as the color play of the embedded minerals make for impressive optics. Similar to wood, fossils have pores and cracks and have to be stabilized prior to processing. In addition, fossilized materials can be dyed, if desired. Whoever wants things to be even more primeval can look for pocket knives with dinosaur bone. They, too, exist.

BRASS, STEEL, ALUMINUM, AND TITANIUM

Brass in the pocket knife industry is primarily only used for liners and bolsters. It still has a kind of iconic status as handle material for Japanese Higonokami knives and French Coursolle knives, mainly depicting motifs with respect to hunting, sports, and mythology on their handle scales.

If stainless steel is used as handle material, the pocket knives usually are either quite small or the scales relatively thin in order to keep the weight low and the handle from being too heavy. During the 1950s and 1960s, gentleman's pocket knives from Solingen with needle-etched handle scales of stainless steel were prospering until they were replaced by the increasingly popular Swiss Army Knives. Together with the knives there vanished the job of the "*Guillochierer*" (needle-etcher), which had even offered the chance for someone to become a master by passing an exam.

Aluminum and titanium today are by far the most commonly used metals, because they are light while also having a high stability. In addition, they are resistant to corrosion and insensitive to temperature changes. With respect to aesthetics, both raw materials have been decisive in the appearance of modern pocket knives during the last couple of decades.

By means of anodic treatment, aluminum can be provided with an abrasion-proof protective layer, which in addition can be dyed as desired. Depending on the mechanical pre-treatment

▶ **MAMMOTH TUSK:** the fossilized finds stem from Northern Siberia.

▶ **MAMMOTH MOLARS:** this exclusive material is used for especially luxurious pocket knives.

(grinding, brushing, abrasive blasting, polishing) attractive surface effects can be created. But even anodized aluminum has the—only cosmetic – disadvantage of not being completely protected from mechanical wear. Since marks and scratches can hardly be avoided, the knife handle will display distinct traces of use over time.

Although titanium in the beginning was a very exclusive material, today it is not even rare among serial knives imported from the Far East. Nevertheless, a titanium folder stays something special because it gives you a totally different feeling of value when taking it in your hand, compared to a knife with scales of stainless steel or aluminum. This pleasant impression is enhanced by the fact that titanium, due to its low thermal conductivity, does not feel as cold to the hand as other metals. Titanium is less sensitive to mechanical stress, compared to aluminum, and especially with sandblasted surfaces, small scratches are almost unobtrusive.

A new trend is using titanium alloys forged together like damascus. Because the alloys change to different colors under the influence of heat, spectacular color patterns are created. As impressive as titanium damascus looks, so complicated and costly is its production. So far there are only a few forges worldwide which have the necessary know-how: Chad Nichols offers titanium damascus under the trading name Moku-Ti; Tom Ferry, Bill Cottrell, and Chuck Bybee called their creation

Timascus. Titanium damascus is normally only used for exclusive mini-series.

PLASTICS AND COMPOSITE MATERIALS

The first synthetic material used in large amounts for the handle scales of pocket knives was celluloid. Invented in 1856, it is seen as the very first of the thermoplastics. The commercial success of the material started in the 1870s. Celluloid could be produced cheaply, could be dyed and shaped at will, and thus was very well suited for the imitation of natural materials such as ivory, amber, horn, tortoiseshell, and mother-of-pearl. Transparent celluloid, in addition, opened up new possibilities for designing handles. In the United States, the brothers Henry and Reuben Landis hit on the idea of putting images underneath transparent celluloid handle scales. They applied for a patent in 1879. A totally new type of pocket knife was born: from then on the handles were decorated with company logos, advertisement texts, Bible quotes, aphorisms, comic heroes, pin-up girls, and many more.

But because celluloid is easily flammable and decomposes over time, it was quickly replaced by other plastics later on. Polyoxymethylene, abbreviated POM, was from 1960 onward, under the trade name Delrin, the new standard material for pocket knife handle scales. It is light, can be shaped and dyed at will, is hard, wear-resistant, and almost inflammable. Since Delrin can also be milled, it was especially used as an authentic looking replacement for bone. Today Delrin is still used sometimes, mostly in milky-looking yellow and beige hues because they are especially sought after by knife enthusiasts.

The number of plastics and composite materials available today for ordinary persons is almost too large to grasp. They all have in common complete corrosion resistance and high mechanical stress endurance. Indeed, quite often additional stabilizing steel liners are left out in the construction of handles. High-quality synthetic handle scales are either made of thermoplastic, fiber-reinforced plastics such as FRN (fiberglass reinforced nylon), which are manufactured by means of injection molding, or they are made of composite materials produced from glass fiber mats and epoxy resin—such as G-10, commonly used for tactical knives. After hardening, G-10 can be sawed and milled.

Depending on the surface treatment (sand-blasting, grinding, polishing), the finish is either smooth or rough.

An especially versatile handle material is micarta. It is a compound of fiber and plastics whose origin traces back to famous inventor George Westinghouse. Micarta is produced by soaking an absorbent carrier material—usually pulp/cellulose or textiles from linen or cotton—with phenolic resin. After the resin has hardened, micarta can be mechanically processed like G-10. Depending on the structure, color, thickness, and layering, micarta can look very different.

Because of its special hi-tech look and the good qualities of the material, modern pocket knives are often provided with handle scales or inlays of carbon fiber. On the surface the typical weaving structure appears to have three-dimensional depth—similar to a hologram.

THE MOST IMPORTANT PLASTICS AND COMPOSITE MATERIALS

Knife manufacturers have access to a wide pallet of synthetic handle materials. The advantages of these materials are their corrosion resistance and mechanical stress endurance.

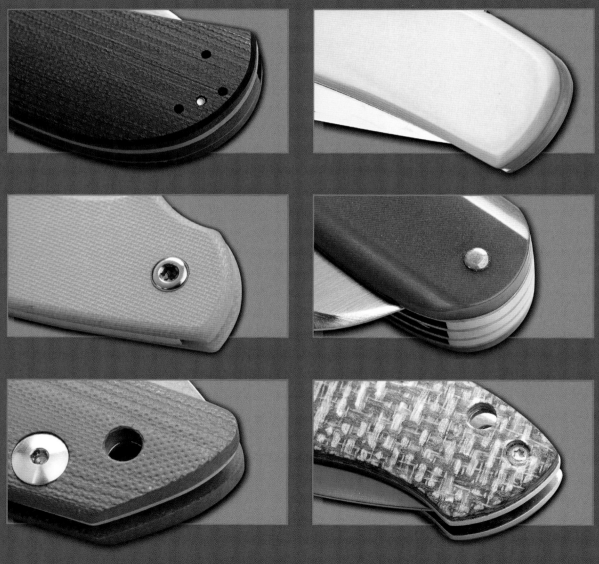

▸ **G-10:** This material, produced of glass fiber mats and epoxy resin, can look very different, depending on dyeing and surface treatment.

▸ **MICARTA:** Depending on carrier material and finish, micarta either looks homogeneous or structured. Fine ivory micarta (on top) looks especially noble.

▸ **CARBON FIBER:** This high-end material is frequently used with modern gentleman's pocket knives.

▸ **ZYTEL:** This glass fiber reinforced nylon material is not very attractive optically, but almost indestructible.

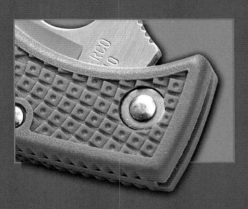

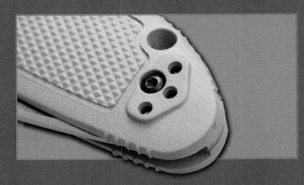

▸ **FRN (fiberglass reinforced nylon):** This plastic, produced by means of injection molding, can be provided with any desired surface structure.

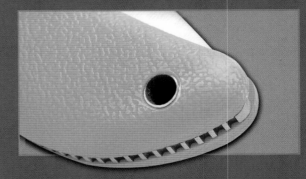

▸ **VALOX:** This thermoplastic material was developed for technical purposes and is mainly used by Benchmade as a handle material.

▸ **KRATON:** This synthetic rubber is a popular handle material for outdoor folders, because it stays slip-proof when wet.

Blade Steel

To say it right away: quite often too much emphasis is put on the choice of the blade steel. Of course, there are significant differences between the individual steel types, and not every type is suitable for the production of knife blades. But since gentleman's pocket knives typically are only used sporadically, it doesn't necessarily have to be provided with the latest super steel. Anyway, the quality of a blade is not only determined by the mixture of alloying elements but also by the heat treatment and the blade geometry. And: how well or badly a blade solves its cutting task is not the least dependent on the goods it has to cut and the more or less experienced handling of the knife by its user.

The most important demands for a blade steel are its cutting abilities, edge retention, corrosion resistance, resistance to wear, and its ability to be sharpened. These qualities, due to the material qualities, are in a complex mutual conflict of objectives. An extremely hard steel type may provide a blade that stays sharp for a long time, but at the same time it is brittle and can cause great trouble with re-sharpening for an average user. A blade of normal carbon steel, on the other hand, is tough and quickly achieves a fine sharpness, but it doesn't stay sharp for a long time and is also prone to corrosion. There is not such a thing as a perfect all-purpose steel. The choice of the blade steel is always a compromise taking the intended use of the knife into account—this holds for manufacturers as well as buyers.

STAINLESS STEEL VERSUS CARBON STEEL

Steel, chemically seen, is an alloy of iron and carbon with the carbon content usually being distinctly less than two percent. The more carbon there is in the steel, the harder the steel is. Mixing in additional alloying elements such as chromium, vanadium, molybdenum, nickel, cobalt, and tungsten changes the chemical and mechanical qualities of the material significantly. Vanadium, for example, even in small amounts, enhances the steel's elasticity.

One of the most important innovations was the invention of stainless steel. But the expressions "stainless" or "non-corrosive," so effective in advertisements, are misleading. Depending on the conditions of the surroundings, even so-called stainless steel oxidizes—just much more slowly than low-alloy steel. It would be more precise to talk of steel with slow corrosion.

At the beginning of the nineteenth century already, the corrosion resistance of iron-chromium alloys was discovered. But it still took a while until the large-scale technical production of corrosion-resistant steel types. On the verge of the First World War it came to an independent parallel invention in three countries: in 1912, the Krupp employees Eduard Maurer and Benno Strauß applied for a patent on stainless steel. At the same time inventor and businessman Elwood Haynes worked on corrosion-resistant steel alloys in the United States. And in England, on August 13, 1913, metallurgist Harry Brearley achieved the decisive breakthrough with an alloying ratio of 12.8 percent of chromium and 0.24 percent of carbon. Steels are seen as "stainless" if they have an alloying ratio of at least twelve percent of chromium.

After World War I, stainless steel was first established for table cutlery; in pocket knife production the new material only played a subordinate role up to the 1940s. To understand this better, you have to know that the production

PATINA AND RUST

While rust is seen as an unwanted appearance of corrosion on blades of carbon steel, many users see the creation of patina as a natural ageing process which gives a knife its individual character. The bluish-black iridescent color changes of the blade are usually the results of contact with acid-containing food. Some knife enthusiasts even promote the creation of patina by covering the blade with mustard, submerging it in vinegar, or putting it into a potato over night. Prior to the invention of electroplating, chemical metal-coloring processes such as burnishing were used to protect blades from rusting.

Rust is a product of oxidation, which is created by the reaction of iron with oxygen. Moisture supports the oxidation. Soon a layer of ferrous oxide and ferric oxide is created on the blade, with the latter causing the ferruginous color. But the oxide layer itself is not suitable as a cohesive protective surface on the blade, but has a porous structure which supports further corrosion until the steel crumbles into rusting dust in the end. Although industry has developed more and more effective stainless steels in the last few decades, carbon steel nevertheless is not outdated. Many users value the property that blades of this steel type can be ground very thin. Thus knives with blades of carbon steel are still produced and sold around the world. In the United States, Great Eastern Cutlery consistently equips the pocket knives of its main brands Tidioute Cutlery and UN-X-LD with blades of carbon steel. The non-corrosive steel 440C is left to a product line of its own. Case, too, offers knife models with blades of non-stainless chromium-vanadium steel. From Japan we know the two rusting steel types Aogami (blue paper steel) and Shirogami (white paper steel) which, by the way, are named after the color of the wrapping material. Carbon steel versions of French Opinel knives are also very popular and heat treatment methods at that time were not nearly as sophisticated as they are today. The material quality quite often still left a lot to be desired, which led to a bad reputation for stainless steel. Queen City Cutlery was one of the first companies to already use stainless steel for a part of their pocket knife blades. But customers accepted the new steel only reluctantly. If the blade was marked with the word "stainless" this even impeded sales success and thus Queen stamped the expression "Queen Steel" onto their stainless blades from the mid-1950s on.

POWDER-METALLURGICAL STEELS

One problem in the production of high-alloy steels in the conventional melting process is how to achieve as homogeneous a structure as possible. What does this mean? The microstructure of steel is—to use an everyday example—gums and teeth: into an elastic-tough basic mass (matrix) tiny but very hard carbon compounds are embedded (carbides). The carbides, which are created by the alloying elements, contribute significantly to the wear resistance of the steel. But if the carbides are very large and distributed unevenly within the matrix, they don't have enough hold in the matrix of the thin blade edge. This leads to nicks under stress loads. Professionals call such a case failure of the cutting edge.

Much finer and more stable carbide structures can be created if the alloying elements are compressed as a powder under high pressure. The different technical processes for creating the powder and subsequent shaping and heat treatment

are the realm of powder metallurgy. Blades of powder-metallurgically created steels (PM steels), because of their homogeneous material structure, have a much more stable cutting edge and are considerably more wear-resistant than blades from steel alloys created in melting processes. But they are a good deal more expensive, too.

A gentleman's pocket knife can be compared to a car with a too powerful engine: actually, you don't need the additional hp, but it is good to know that the power reserve is at hand, in case you should require it in an emergency.

AESTHETICS IN STEEL: DAMASCUS

Damascus steel is seen as the perfected art of forging. A special property of damascus steel is its decorative patterns, which result from the alternating layers of two or more different steel types. The prevalent idea that the Medieval smiths of edged weapons combined hard and soft layers of steel in order to forge sword blades which were both wear-resistant and flexible belongs in the realm of myth.

As a cheap alternative to real damascus steel, in Solingen the damascus effect was copied already from the seventeenth century onward by etching intertwined patterns onto the surface of monosteel blades. This decoration technique known in German as "*Damaszierung*" was used until the 1950s, but lost more and more of its importance later on.

Real damascus steel is produced by stacking layers of differently alloyed steels to form a so-called billet, which is fixed on one side with a welding seam. Afterwards, the damascus billet is heated up in the forging fire in order to weld the layers together. By well-aimed hammer blows the billet is repeatedly stretched out, then notched and folded again. Instead of the physically demanding way of working with forging hammers and anvil, air hammers are used nowadays. Despite the support by machines, the smith has to shape the workpiece with skillful visual judgment.

If the damascus billet is only shaped by folding, layered damascus is created, which displays an irregular pattern of lines on its surface (wild damascus). If the steel is twisted, wavelike or ripply patterns can be created (twisted damascus). Further processing techniques such as punching create artsy, delicate ornamentation (roses, pyramids, diamonds, herring bone patterns, and more) or spectacular structures (mosaic and explosion pattern damascus). Finally, the blade made of damascus is etched in order to enhance the optical contrast between the individual steel layers.

In Germany, high-quality damascus steel is made by experienced smiths such as Markus Balbach and Achim Wirtz. In the United States

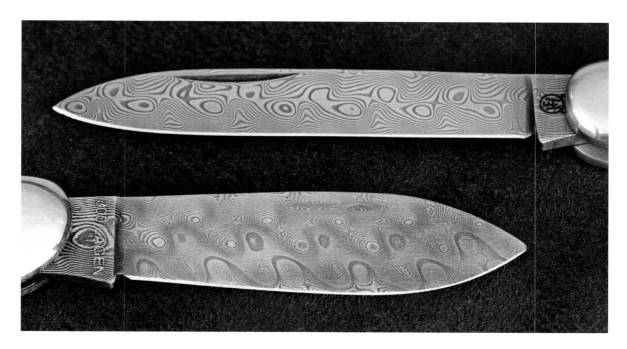

▶ **PRECIOUS GEMS:** these blades consist of 100-layer and 300-layer damascus by Markus Balbach.

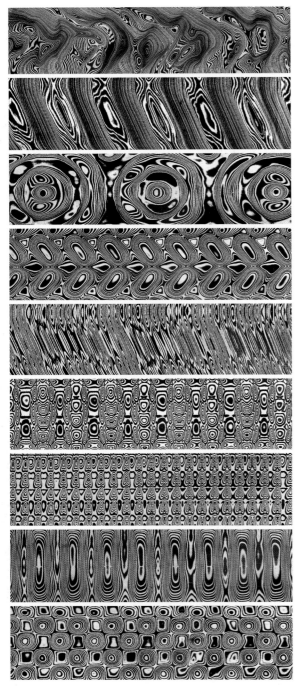

▸ **FROM GEOMETRICAL TO PSYCHEDELIC:** Damasteel produces PM-damascus with many different patterns.

Chad Nichols has made his mark with creatively patterned damascus steels which are now imported even by European companies such as Böker and Lion Steel for the production of pocket knife blades.

Today, non-stainless as well as stainless damascus is produced. The founders of the Swedish company Damasteel revolutionized the century-old technique of making damascus steel when they developed a patented method for producing powder-metallurgical damascus steel in the mid-1990s. This PM-damascus, which is offered with many attractive embellishments, is in high demand; knife companies from North Sweden to Southern France process it to make blades of high-quality serial knives.

A specialty is the suminagashi laminated steel of Japan: a multi-layered decorative damascus is forged onto both sides of a blade core of hard monosteel (e.g. VG-10). Suminagashi means, freely translated, "flowing watercolor" and is derived from the similarity of the damascus pattern with the ornamentation of Japanese mottled paper traditionally produced in a water bath. The pocket knives of the Japanese brands Mcusta are often provided with optically very intriguing suminagashi blades.

HARDNESS MEASUREMENT ACCORDING TO ROCKWELL

The steel's hardness is an important indicator— although not the only one—for the quality of a blade. But in general it can be said: the harder the steel, the more wear-resistant the blade is. This means the blade edge keeps its sharpness longer with a hard steel, compared to a soft steel.

Various measuring techniques were developed in order to exactly determine the hardness of a workpiece. For blade steel, the hardness is measured according to the Rockwell scale, named after the American engineer Stanley Rockwell. Described in a simplified way, the measurement is done this way: a calibrated testing device impresses a rounded diamond cone into the blade with a determined force for a defined time span. The depth of the diamond's impression is seen as measurement for the hardness, which is converted into HRC according to a mathematical formula ("HR" means "Hardness Rockwell" and "C" stands for the method).

Some producers do this test with each blade, others only for random samples. The typical area of hardness for knife blades is between 52 and 67 HRC, the latter being a rare extreme. For daily use, a pocket knife with a hardness between 56 and 60 HRC is totally sufficient.

▶ **SUSPICIOUS DENT:** the tiny depression in the blade is the result of the hardness check.

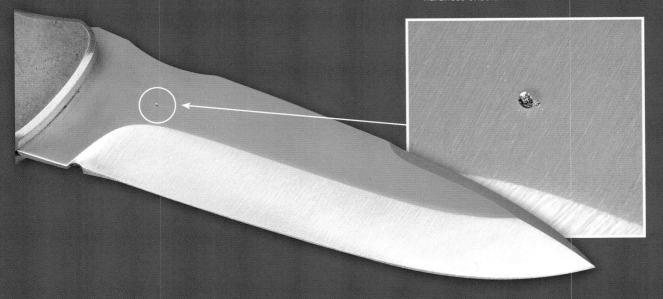

THE MOST COMMONLY USED BLADE STEELS FOR POCKET KNIVES

The extreme multitude of steel types used by knife producers is confusing for ordinary people. In addition, the orientation is impeded by different national and producer-specific naming standards. The following list contains a selection of the most commonly used blade steels. With the exception of 1095, XC70, and D2, these are all stainless steels.

1095, XC70

Hidden behind these names is a non-stainless carbon steel with the numbers hinting at the carbon content (0.95 and 0.7 percent respectively). Other carbon contents are also quite common (e.g. 1075, 1085, XC90).

1.4116

This German material number relates to a blade steel commonly used in Solingen's cutlery industry. Usually it is hardened to between 56 and 58 HRC. Alongside the steels 1.4110 and 1.4034 it is preferred for pocket hunting knives.

12C27, 14C28N

The Swedish company Sandvik developed both steel types especially for knife blades.12C27 has become a quasi-standard for French pocket knives. 14C28N is somewhat harder and more corrosion-resistant than 12C27.

154-CM

This steel, produced by the American company Crucible, is 440C enriched in molybdenum. Prior to the era of PM steels it was seen as premium steel with especially good corrosion resistance. The chemically identical but powder-metallurgically produced CPM-154 is the modern counterpart to 154-CM.

420

This steel today can only be seen with very cheap pocket knives. If the only designation is just "stainless," the steel in question is usually 420 or 440A. Because it is very soft, its edge-retention leaves a lot to be desired. This is different to 420HC ("HC" stands for high carbon content) which has a good hardness with accordingly good heat treatment.

440C

While the variants A and B of the 440-series can today only be found in the lower price segment, 440C is still used for high-quality pocket knives. If 440 is given as the only designation, usually 440A is the used steel.

8CR13MOV

This cryptic abbreviation listing the alloying elements names a blade steel which can often be found with knives produced in China. It has acceptable material properties and is easy to sharpen, even for untrained persons.

ATS-34

In the 1970s, American knifemaker Bob Loveless made this steel, produced by Hitachi, popular within the knife scene. ATS-34 is chemically identical to 154-CM. A powder-metallurgically created variant of this steel is marketed under the name RWL-34.

AUS-8

The Japanese steel AUS-8 is of good average quality, comparable to the Chinese steel 8Cr13MoV. Because of its excellent ratio of cost and performance it is used quite often.

D2

With a chromium content of eleven percent, this tool steel is just below the threshold of stainlessness and thus is sometimes called "semi-stainless." It is especially valued for its wear resistance.

LAMINATED STEEL

For steels of several layers, a cutting layer of hard steel is combined with flanks of flexible steel in order to achieve as high a stability of the blade as is possible. Fällkniven, for example, uses a laminated steel with a core of the exclusive PM steel SGPS (Super Gold Powder Steel) having a hardness of 62 HRC onto which layers of the rather unspectacular steel 420J are added on both sides.

N690

This steel, developed by the Austrian company Böhler, is a high-quality all-round steel and is preferably used by European knife producers.

S30V, S35VN

For a long time S30V was seen as second to none with respect to PM steels for pocket knives. This blade steel became especially popular because of the knives of Chris Reeve, who was also contributing to its development. Its successor S35VN also was created due to an idea of Chris Reeve. It has an additional niobium content, which has a finer matrix and is easier to process. In practice, both steels only differ slightly. Because they are quite expensive, they are only used for upmarket knives. The steel types S60V and S90V of the same product family are only rarely used.

VG10

This high-quality steel is often used for the knives of Spyderco produced in Japan. It offers an excellent combination of easy re-sharpening, edge retention, wear resistance, and corrosion resistance.

ZDP-189

This knife steel was developed by Hitachi in cooperation with the Japanese knifemaker Katsumi Kitano and distinguishes itself by its high carbon and chromium content. Blades of ZDP-189 are extremely wear-resistant because they can be hardened up to the impressive value of 67 HRC. Beginners with no experience with respect to re-sharpening should use steel types which are less hard.

Locking Mechanisms

To make the handling of pocket knives safer and more secure, many mechanisms were invented during the past centuries capable of locking the unfolded blade. The first step was the invention of the back spring, which impedes folding the blade without really locking it. These so-called slipjoint folders are still very popular, all the more since they can be carried in public without legal restrictions in most countries.

The spectrum of locking mechanisms used today is wide. Some mechanisms are specific to the producer, such as the axis lock developed by

BACK LOCK (LOCKBACK, BACK LOCKING MECHANISM)

The back lock is a well-proven locking mechanism which, although it wasn't invented by the American company Buck, nevertheless achieved great popularity because of the legendary model 110. The locking mechanism consists of two components. A locking lever positioned in the center is kept under tension by means of a spring anchored at the rear handle end. At its front end, the lever with its so-called hammer rests in a locking recession of the tang. In order to open the lock, the lever is pressed downwards against the spring's pressure. The depicted Spyderco model has a shortened lever.

1. spring
2. locking lever
3. hammer
4. locking recession

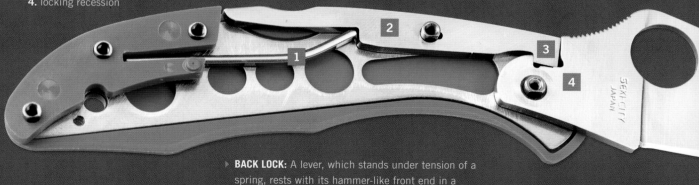

▶ **BACK LOCK:** A lever, which stands under tension of a spring, rests with its hammer-like front end in a corresponding recess of the blade tang.

Benchmade or Cold Steel's Tri-Ad lock. Ingenious inventors surprise the world with ever new mechanisms which are mostly limited to a few folding knife models. The locking mechanisms which are most widespread and not limited to specific companies are the back lock, frame lock, and liner lock.

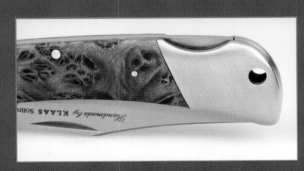

▶ **CLASSIC CONSTRUCTION:** A recess shaped like a half moon at the handle's rear end gives access to part of the lever so it can be pressed downwards.

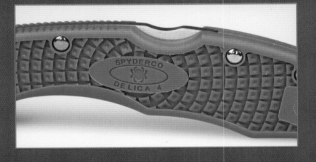

▶ **MID-BACK LOCK:** Because of the shortened lever, the pressure point is in the center of the handle's back. The additional small indentation is called "David Boye dent" (after the knifemaker with the same name).

▶ **WITHOUT RECESS:** The locking lever protrudes beyond the handle's rear end.

▶ **PROTRUDING:** The so-called trigger can also be used well with gloves.

FRAME LOCK

This locking mechanism consists of an elastic lock bar (retaining spring) which is part of the handle frame. In locked position a small metal ball (detent ball), which is impressed in the retaining spring, locks into a small indentation of the blade tang and thus prevents inadvertent opening of the blade. When the blade is in working position, the retaining spring rests under the knife tang, blocking it this way. To unlatch the lock, the retaining spring is pushed sideways and the blade is folded. The mechanism was made popular by Chris Reeves under the name Integral Lock.

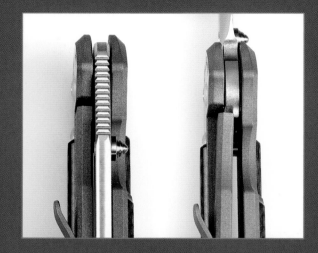

▶ **FRAME LOCK:** The retaining spring is part of the handle frame which is usually made of titanium or stainless steel.

LINER LOCK

This mechanism is used for folding knives whose handles consist of liners and handle scales. As with the frame lock, a retaining spring arrests the blade in open position. The elastic lock bar is part of the liner—thus the name for this locking mechanism. The liner lock mechanism was developed by the American knifemaker Michael Walker.

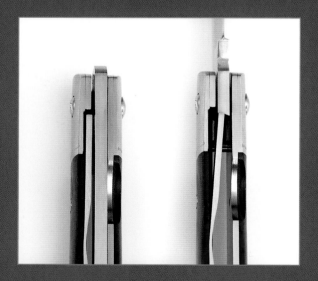

▶ **LINER LOCK:** An elastic part of the liner blocks the knife tang.

BUTTON LOCK

The button lock can be found especially with pocket knives of the company William Henry. But other manufacturers as well use this locking mechanism for some model or other of their product range. The system consists of an elastically mounted bolt which can be pressed downwards through a drill hole in the handle scale. The bolt has a widened base which fits into a corresponding recess of the knife tang and this way arrests the opened blade. If the bolt is pressed downwards, the part with the smaller diameter releases the knife tang and the blade can be closed. When the blade is in closed position, the bolt rests in a second recess shaped in such a way that the knife tang slides over the bolt's base automatically—without additional pressure on the button— thus pressing it downwards.

▷ **BUTTON LOCK:** The widened base of an elastically mounted bolt latches on a corresponding recess in the knife tang.

HOW IT WORKS

▷ **WITH FOLDED BLADE:** a coil spring presses the bolt into a recess of the knife tang shaped in such a way that the blade is held back in the handle without arresting it.

▷ **WHEN OPENING THE BLADE:** without having to press the button, the blade tang slides over the bolt's base and presses it downwards against the coil spring.

▷ **WITH OPEN BLADE:** the basis of the bolt locks in a recess of the knife tang made for this purpose, thus blocking the tang. The lock can only be undone by pressing the bolt downwards from the outside.

VIROBLOC (TWIST LOCK)

One of the simplest and at the same time most reliable locking mechanisms is the virobloc system, which was invented by Opinel and is based on the twist lock of the Nontron knives. In the area of the axis pin, the wooden handle is strengthened by a metal ferrule. On top of this, there is a pivoted sleeve which is made of metal, too. This securing ring locks the blade in open as well as closed position.

▶ **SIMPLE BUT SAFE:** a pivoted metal sleeve locks the blade in closed position.

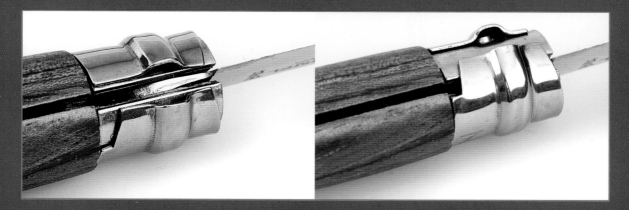

▶ **IN WORKING POSITION:** The opened blade is locked by a turn of the metal ring.

ABCs of Blade Shapes

Shape and grind of a blade determine its cutting properties. The blade shapes most commonly used for gentleman's pocket knives are drop point, spear point, and clip point. The other shapes are mostly used in the blade ensemble of multi-bladed American pocket knives. The most commonly used grinds are flat grind and hollow grind.

BLADE CONTOURS

▶ **DROP POINT BLADE:** typical for this blade shape are the slight curve of the blade back descending towards the tip and the cutting edge belly. Both characteristics turn the drop point blade into a good all-round utility.

▶ **SPEAR POINT BLADE:** for this symmetrical blade shape, the blade tip is positioned centered on the longitudinal axis of the blade. In Solingen it is thus also called "mittelspitze Klinge" ("blade with centered point").

▶ **PEN BLADE:** this blade is a small version of the spear point blade which in former times was mostly used for sharpening quills and pencils.

▶ **CLIP POINT BLADE:** the special trait of this blade shape is the concave curve of the blade back, which looks as if part of the blade has been cut off ("clipped"). This curved part of the blade back is usually provided with a false edge.

▸ **CALIFORNIA CLIP POINT BLADE:** this special shape is an elongated clip point blade whose contours are supposed to be similar to those of the state of California.

▸ **SHEEPSFOOT BLADE:** this shape, also called lambsfoot blade, has a straight cutting edge and a back which abruptly drops downwards to the cutting edge, thus avoiding a distinct blade tip.

▸ **COPING BLADE:** this blade, related to the sheepsfoot blade, initially was used by carpenters and joiners for scribing marks into wooden workpieces.

▸ **HAWKBILL BLADE:** this blade, also called "pruning blade," is especially common with garden knives, but is also useful for drawing cuts (e.g. for slitting open sacks).

▸ **SPEY BLADE:** this blade shape, also called castrating blade, is almost exclusively found with traditional American pocket knives. Initially it was developed for castrating farm animals.

▸ **WHARNCLIFF BLADE:** similar to the sheepsfoot blade, the cutting edge is straight, but here the curve of the blade back starts already close to the handle.

▸ **LONG SPEY BLADE:** the long spey blade is typically one of the two blades of a trapper pocket knife.

Blade Cross Sections

▶ **FLAT GRIND:** blades with a flat grind have a wedge-shaped cross section and can be used for almost any cutting task. The grind either leads directly up to the blade back ("full flat grind") or ends close to it. The secondary bevel is distinguished from the primary bevel by its more obtuse angle.

▶ **SCANDINAVIAN GRIND:** this is a variation of the flat grind with the grind starting usually at a third of the blade's height above the cutting edge or at most halfway up. A secondary bevel is usually dispensed with; the grind is done "to zero," as is customarily said.

▶ **HOLLOW GRIND:** this grind, also called concave grind, is distinguished by its more or less inwards curved flanks. Because of this blade geometry, the blade penetrates especially easily into the materials to be cut. Because of the large amount of removed stock, blade and cutting edge are not very stable.

▶ **SPHERICAL GRIND:** characteristic for this grind, also called convex grind, are the outwards bulging blade flanks which provide high stability to the cutting edge. Because of the special blade geometry, a convex ground blade acts rather splitting than cutting.

CHAPTER 4

STYLES AND TRADITIONS

Cutting the French Way

"How should someone govern a country which has 246 different types of cheese?," French president Charles de Gaulle sighed during an interview in 1946. The vivid regional cultures of France not only manifest themselves in wine and cheese, the Grand Nation also possesses a rich tradition of regional pocket knives which is unique worldwide. About fifty different models are still produced by several manufacturers today. A stately number of so-called neo-regional pocket knives can be added to them. Two knives of regional origin—the Laguiole and the Opinel—achieved the status of national symbols which are almost as famous as the Eiffel Tower.

From medieval times to the nineteenth century several places existed in France where edged weapons and cutlery were produced. In addition to sword- and knifesmiths in the well-known towns Thiers and Laguioule, there were also smiths in Châtellerault, Langres, Nogent, Nontron, Paris, and St. Etienne. Some of the towns lost their importance early. The art of knife forging, for example, in Sauveterre-de-Rouergue was at its zenith during the fifteenth century, but this era was already gone about one hundred years later.

In the course of time the production of cutlery centered more and more in Thiers, which calls itself "*capitale de la coutellerie*" (capital of cutlery).

REGIONAL KNIFE DIVERSITY

Almost all traditional French pocket knives are rooted in the living environment of the rural population. The farmers, herders, vintners, and miners needed reliable and inexpenisve knives for work and daily chores. At many places characteristic knife companies were founded whose names still refer to their regional distribution—not necessarily to the place of their creation, because most knives were indeed manufactured in Thiers.

In the northeast of France the folding knives Donjon, Gouttière, Langres, Tiré droit, and Tonneau belong to the rural culture of Burgundy. They all have a large sheepsfoot blade and are used for work in the garden, vineyard, and kitchen. In the Alsace the Alsacien is widespread. Because of the club shaped widening of the handle, it is also called Massu. The Mineur bears the name of an occupational group: once it was the work knife of the miners in the coal mines in the east of

▶ **FRENCH TRADITIONAL KNIVES:** the Nontron (left) is seen as one of the oldest knives of France. The Douk-Douk (center) has been produced almost without change since 1929. The Coursolle knives in production since 1902— also called Sujet knives—are equipped with embossed brass scales showing motifs of country life, sports, or mythology (at right).

▶ **TWO ICONS:** the Laguiole and the Opinel are the most renowned international representatives of French knife culture.

France. The knife types Berger and Piétin with two blades could be found wherever sheep and cattle were bred. The smaller, curved blade was used for cutting the hooves. The fine Navette, usually provided with several blades, was the gentleman's knife of the successful townsman, in comparison.

The southeast of France knows alpine as well as maritime knives. The Alpin served well for the mountain farmers of Savoy. Towards the end of the nineteenth century, it stimulated the young Joseph Opinel to construct a cheaper variant of

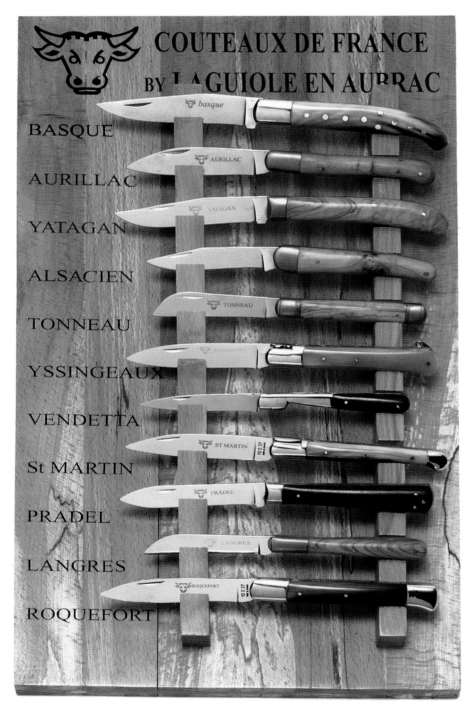

COUTEAUX DE FRANCE
BY LAGUIOLE EN AUBRAC

BASQUE

AURILLAC

YATAGAN

ALSACIEN

TONNEAU

YSSINGEAUX

VENDETTA

St MARTIN

PRADEL

LANGRES

ROQUEFORT

▸ **LIVING TRADITION:** the company Laguiole en Aubrac produces a series of classic regional knives in addition to the Laguiole knives.

this knife with a twist lock instead of the back spring. The Montpellier was the all-purpose knife for sailors who not only used it for cutting rope and sailcloth but also for their meals. The slim Vendetta with its characteristic "*taille de guêpe*" (wasp waist) is seen as the typical Corsican knife, although it was exclusively produced in Thiers. An authentic knife forged by the village smiths on Corsica (and still made there) is the Corse Amicu which is used by the herders on this island.

The Capucin stems from the country's southwest. It competes with the Nontron with respect to which is the oldest folding knife of France. The name is derived from the shape of the handle's end, which is similar to the headdress of Capuchin monks. The models Agenais, Saint-Amant, and Bonnet, which have their home in the southwest of France as well, belong to a family of knives whose special trait is a blade shaped like a sage leaf. The Boule and the Basque Yatagan are not only widespread in the Spanish Basque region but also in the French regions adjacent to the Pyrenees. Other regional knives of the Southwest are the Garonnais and the Violon. The Châtellerault of the small town with the same name is unusual insofar as it wasn't a work knife of the rural population but a knife of the aristocrats made of precious materials with elaborate ornamentations. Quite often it was their symbol of status.

In the northwest of France, especially in the coastal regions, the London, a sailor's knife which probably originated in England, became established. But it was not only a constant companion of sailors, the peasant population as well soon appreciated its advantages. Other knives typical for the region of the Northwest are the elegant Rouennais, the Corse, the Poisson Culot, the Fénérol, and the small-format Queue de Poisson, which was especially popular with women. In the nineteenth century, the Pradel was created after a model from

▶ **CORSE AMICU:** the rustic Corsican shepherd's knife falls outside the typical scope of slim French regional knives.

Sheffield. At the beginning of the twentieth century it spread from Brittany and Normandy throughout all of France and at that time enjoyed a similar popularity as the Opinel or Laguiole nowadays.

The highest density of regional pocket knives, of course, can be found in the heart of France, the various regions of the Massif Central. Here not only the legendary Laguiole was created but many other models as well. The Yssingeaux, the Issoire, the Roquefort, and the Saint-Martin all belong to the surroundings of the Laguiole knife. The Aveyronnais is sometimes called the "Laguiole des pauvres," the Laguiole of the poor. But actually it is just a version of the famous knife without embellishments and is even preferred by some enthusiasts because of its simple design. The models Aurillac and Salers stem from the volcanic region of the Cantal. They were the tools of farmers and cattle breeders.

THE MYTH LAGUIOLE

Many myths are woven around the history of the Laguiole's creation. Around 1829, it is said, the young knifesmith Pierre Jean Calmels (1813–1876) was the first to make a Laguiole. The village Laguiole is located on the Western border of the elevated plain Aubrac in the Massif Central, a sparsely populated area which then as well as today lives from agriculture. The knife was meant as an all-round utility knife for the farmers and herders of the region, who up to then had used fixed blades.

It is a widespread story that Calmels was inspired by the Spanish Navaja when designing the knife, but the story lacks all plausibility. The alleged Spanish template and the initial Laguiole don't share any more similarity than the fact that both are folding knives with a handle and a single blade.

The first Laguiole knife was much simpler than the common knives of today. It did not have the curved handle shape and the typical Yatagan blade, but also lacked bolsters and the embellishments of the back spring. Because of its straight shape, the early Laguiole knife is also called "*Laguiole droit*." As handle material, bone or the horn tips of cattle raised in the Aubrac were used. The processing of the knives was also not at the level of today's quality standards. For the farmers the affordability of the knife was more important than a polished finish.

During the 1830s and 1840s, more families from Laguiole and the neighboring villages participated in the production of folding knives, which soon became popular beyond the regional borders. When Pierre Jean Calmels, as the first knifesmith of Laguiole, was awarded a medal in 1868, suddenly the attention of the knife producers in Thiers was attracted. At that time a development started which led to an unforgiving conflict between both places. The fact that many people of the poor rural population fled to the larger cities during the nineteenth century also added to the popularity of this knife type. When the Parisians discovered the useful knives of their immigrated fellow citizens of the Aveyron, the fame of the knives quickly spread throughout the capital and other parts of the country.

More awards followed the first one; the common

▶ **SPLENDID SPECIMENS:** these Laguiole knives are from the manufactory Forge de Laguiole, which has produced the famous knives at their place of origin since 1987, and runs a forge there.

▶ **ADVENTUROUS:** the Forge de Laguiole is known for always following new ways—such as with the handle scales of stabilized stone depicted here.

FLY OR BEE?

The emblematic trait of any Laguiole knife is the bee. Or is it a fly? The confusion, which is created over and over again, depends on the fact that the widened front of the spring is called "*la mouche*" in the professional jargon of the French knife-smiths, which translates as "the fly." But this is a technical expression that doesn't have anything to do with the insect. Initially, this part of the spring was not decorated at all. Only around 1880, did makers start to embellish the front end of the spring. In the beginning, flower motifs such as the *fleur-de-lis* were especially popular. Only Jules Calmels, grandchild of Pierre Jean Calmels, decorated the front end of the spring with a bee ("*l'abeille*") as late as 1908.

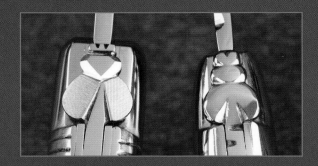

By the way: for high-quality Laguiole knives, spring and bee are forged of a single piece of steel, with the bee filed manually out of the material. Cheap wares can be recognized by the bee consisting of an embossed and punched-out piece of metal which has been soldered or welded onto the spring.

interest in this knife type grew and the knifesmiths in and around Laguiole were unable to serve the

▶ **GUILLOCHE:** the delicate decorations are carved out of the backspring's material with files and needles.

increasing demand. The powerful competition from Thiers stepped into the breach. At the end of the nineteenth century, the production of Laguiole knives went over more and more to Thiers until, at the end of World War I, the last family business vanished from Laguiole.

When the fabrication of Laguiole knives at the place of origin was revived by the foundation of the Forge de Laguiole in 1987, the old competitive relation between Laguiole and Thiers was also renewed again. The same strong rivalry exists between the Forge de Laguiole and the manufactory Laguiole en Aubrac located in the neighboring Espalion. In focus there is always the question of authenticity of the famous knife. Can a Laguiole knife produced outside Laguiole also be called such? Since Laguiole had missed the opportunity in the past to legally protect design and name of the knife, legal clarification of the issue is not to be expected. But because in Thiers as well as Espalion Laguiole knives have been manufactured since the nineteenth century, Laguiole has to live with the fact that companies such as Fontenille Pataud, Robert David, and Laguiole en Aubrac continue this tradition in the best manner.

The real danger comes from the outside anyway: poor-quality knives in Laguiole style which are mass-produced in Pakistan, India, and China have flooded the market for years already and damage the reputation of all serious Laguiole manufacturers in France.

A KNIFE AS MEMORIAL: LE THIERS

The city of Thiers for many centuries was the center of French cutlery production. But while

▶ **LE THIERS:** this classic example of the Coutellerie Chambriard is provided with an additional corkscrew.

▶ **THREE INTERPRETATIONS OF THE THIERS KNIFE BY CLAUDE DOZORME:** the producers have large artistic leeway for their creations.

the name "Laguiole" became the synonym for the knives produced there, for a long time there was no representative knife with the name "Thiers." This changed in 1993. In this year for the first time the Confrérie du Couteau met at Thiers, a small group of knifemakers and enthusiasts who decided to honor their city with a memorial in the form of a knife. It was finished by November 7, 1994: "Le Thiers" was introduced to the public.

Back then not only a prototype was made, but basic rules were set as well for everybody who wants to market a knife under the name "Le Thiers." Among the rules was also complying with certain quality standards as well as the obligation to produce the knives within the region. In addition, every new interpretation of the Thiers knife has to be shown to a jury for an assessment. If the examination is passed, production is allowed, and it can display the desired "Le Thiers" logo. In the meantime, the Confrérie has about 200 members with fifty companies and knifemakers registering around 500 variants of the Le Thiers pocket knives in recent years.

NEO-REGIONAL POCKET KNIVES

Many classic regional knives look back on a long history. But in recent years, too, new knife models have been created in various areas of France. Since they don't yet have the patina of time-honored things, they are called neo-regional. These new creations are usually only made by a single knifemaker or small family business, which means they'll probably never get the same fame as the Laguiole. But they nevertheless have an original appeal because each of these knives has a history which has to be uncovered.

LE TRAPPEUR: Charmbriard produces the Le Thiers in a large version as a pocket hunting knife.

▶ **A SELECTION OF NEO-REGIONAL POCKET KNIVES (FROM TOP TO BOTTOM):** Le Cabos (Jean Paul Tisseyre), Le Morta (Atelier JHP),
L'Ariégeois (Coutellerie Savignac), Le Sauveterre (Guy Vialis), Le Camembert (Guy Vialis), L'Arconsat (Jean-Claude Laforet),
Le Nîmois (Coutellerie Domingo), Le Nogentais (Lame Nogentaise), Le Camarguais (Coutellerie Le Camarguais).

Bella Italia

Similar to France, the production of cutlery in Italy initially was distributed over several regions until finally a concentration in the small towns Scarperia and Maniago took place.

MANIAGO

In Maniago cutlery has been produced since medieval times. The town in the region of Friuli in the country's northeast is often called Italy's Solingen.

While Scarperia today almost exclusively hosts traditional manufactories, the companies located in Maniago, such as Fantoni, Fox Knives, LionSteel, Maserin, and Tecnocut, have state-of-the-art technical equipment at their disposal. Their know-how concerning production is increasingly in demand by partner companies of Europe and even the United States, who have parts of their product portfolio produced in Maniago.

▸ **VIEW OF THE WORKSHOP OF THE COLTELLERIA SALADINI IN SCARPERIA:** processing traditional materials such as wood and horn demand the highest standards with respect to skills in manual production.

For their own product lines the factories cooperate with renowned knife designers. Modern folders for tactical purposes, outdoors, and daily use are created this way. And: each of the mentioned manufacturers has at least one elegant gent's pocket knife in the portfolio.

SCARPERIA

The medieval-looking village Scarperia north of Florence is well-known for its excellent blades since the fifteenth century. But during the past century the tradition of craftsmanship was almost lost. Since the 1980s, many different efforts have been made to keep its venerable heritage: historic

studies were promoted, exhibitions organized, and after several years of preparation, even a museum was founded in 1999. The museum, which is housed in the Palazzo dei Vicari, documents the traditional production of cutlery in Scarperia.

Today, several manufactories produce cutlery of all kinds in this village in the Mugello Valley.

▶ **GENTLEMAN'S FOLDER OF THE BRAND VIPER:** by the combination of classic design, traditional olive wood, and modern steel timelessly beautiful pocket knives are created.

In addition to kitchen knives and table wares, especially traditional regional knives of Italy are made here in manual work. The three most well-known family businesses that also successfully market their products abroad are Berti, ConAz (better known under the brand Consigli), and Saladini.

ITALY'S REGIONAL KNIVES

The canon of Italian regional knives is somewhat more manageable than the multitude of French knives. Here, as well as in France, the origins can mostly be found in the rural culture of farmers and herders. Traditionally horn and olive wood are used as handle materials, but sometimes exotic wood types are used as well. The knives introduced here are just a selection.

▸ **RASOLINO TAGLIASIGARI:** the design, which imitates a razor, stems from Sicily. When pocket knives with pointed blades were forbidden at the beginning of the twentieth century, this knife type spread all over Italy. By means of the recess in the handle's center, the knife can be used for cutting cigars.

▸ **ANCONETANO:** the knife originates in the Adriatic coastal region around the harbor city Ancona. A small recess at the handle's end reminds one of its origin as a fisher's knife. The recess was an aid in repairing fishing nets.

▶ **GOBBO:** the name of this knife is derived from the Italian word for "hunchbacked" which hints at its curved shape. The Gobbo was very popular in Italy during the nineteenth century.

▶ **MAREMMANO A FOGLIA:** this knife is named after the coastal area Maremma including southern Tuscany and parts of the northern Latium. The add-on "a foglia" refers to the leaf-shaped blade.

▶ **CALABRESE:** ss the name already suggests, this knife has its origin in the region Calabria, in the boot's tip of Italy. Its elegant shape is similar to that of the Fiorentino.

▶ **RONCOLA:** the Roncola undoubtedly has its origin in winegrowing and horticulture. Billhook-shaped tools of this kind are known in many countries since the Roman era.

▶ **ZUAVA:** this traditional working knife could be found in the entire Tuscany area up to the nineteenth century and is seen as the typical Scarperia knife. In contrast to other regional knives, the handle structure is strengthened with steel liners, which were a novelty at that time.

▶ **MOZETTA:** like the Rasolino, this knife as well lacks a distinct blade tip. When pointed pocket knife blades were prohibited by means of the Giolitti Law in 1908, these knives could still be carried.

Typical German?

Is there a typical German pocket knife? When taking the deep roots of an Opinel within the French culture or the iconic status of the Swiss Army Knife as a measure, then the answer is a clear "no." Nevertheless, there are a few traditional pocket knife models that were either invented in Germany or mostly produced at Solingen.

MERCATOR KNIVES

Historically seen, the first knife to be mentioned here is the Mercator knife, which will be introduced in more detail elsewhere in this book. Heinrich Kaufmann developed this knife in 1867, as a simple and elegant all-round knife. During the era of the German empire the Mercator knife became widespread, which later led to its popular name "*Kaiser-Wilhelm-Messer*" (Emperor Wilhelm Knife). It is still valued by enthusiasts, but almost unknown outside the world of knives.

"AUTO" WITH LEVER LOCK

At the beginning of the nineteenth century, inventors in Sheffield, Solingen, and elsewhere experimented with different spring-assisted mechanisms in order to open pocket knives with a single hand. Around mid-century, in sales

▶ **CLASSICS IN A MODERN OUTFIT:** the handles of Mercator knives of the "Trendy Fashion" series made by the company Otter-Messer are provided with lively color motifs.

documents of Solingen, the expression "Aufspringmesser" ("burst-open knife") is mentioned, which means that marketable products must have already existed at that time.

Among the many ingenious automatic knives with sliders, push buttons, levers, and other kinds of trigger, in German one mechanism became established and is still in use—especially by the company Hubertus. These pocket knives known as "Springer" are provided with a leaf spring which is mounted lengthwise on the handle's surface and keeps an arresting bolt under tension, which in turn blocks the blade in closed position. Within the handle there is an ejecting spring which lets the blade fly out of the handle sideways as soon as the bolt is lifted, which is done by means of a small lever. To prevent unintentional activation of the mechanism, the lever can be folded towards

the front. The lever is thus activator as well as safety at the same time (lever lock). In open position, the blade is arrested by the bolt, too. In order to close the knife, the bolt has to be lifted by means of the lever. Then the blade can be pressed into the handle against the resistance of the ejection spring until the locking bolt latches again.

The "jumping" mechanism is sometimes wrongly attributed to the American inventor and businessman George Schrade, who applied for several patents regarding automatic knives in the years before and after 1900. Fact is, we are unable to retrace who invented this special mechanism or who used it first. Apparently it was never patented. In any case, many renowned producers of cutlery in Solingen used it up to the mid-twentieth century.

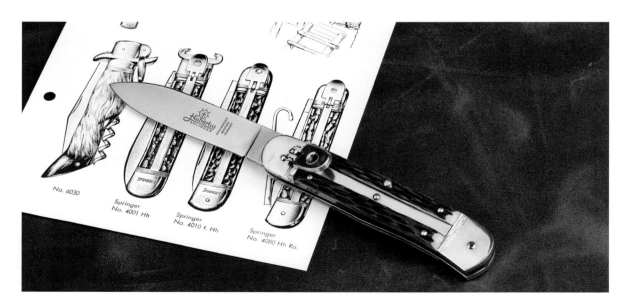

TYPICAL SOLINGEN: the company Hubertus offers "autos" in various sizes and versions.

"POCKET SLAUGHTERING KNIFE" (SODBUSTER)

German models most probably inspired the pocket knife type that is known as "Sodbuster" in the United States. While the knife type itself is much older, the name was coined with the model "Sod Buster"—written as two words—which was introduced by Case at the end of the 1960s. In pattern books of Solingen from the early twentieth century onward knives of this kind are called "*Taschenschlachtmesser*" ("pocket slaughtering knives") or "*Notschlachtmesser*" ("emergency slaughtering knife"). As the names already hint, these robust folding knives, mostly supplied with a back lock, were mainly used as working knives in agriculture and cattle breeding. They are still produced by several companies of Solingen and are even available in very handy versions that can be used as gentleman's knives.

The American expression "sodbuster," by the way, is based on a depreciative expression for those American settlers who purchased land after the Homestead Act of 1862. Because the land outside of the already settled area was wild prairie, the farmers had to laboriously break open ("to bust") the turf ("sod") in order to gain areas useful for agriculture.

▶ **SODBUSTER KNIFE FROM THE PRODUCTION OF FRIEDRICH OLBERTZ**: in pattern books of Solingen these pocket knives are listed under the names "*Taschenschlachtmesser*" or "*Notschlachtmesser*."

▸ **GOOD HUNTING:** this pocket hunting knife with five parts is a model of Solingen's company Diefenthal.

HUNTING POCKET KNIFE
WITH STAG HANDLE SCALES

A special niche is formed by the multi-bladed pocket hunting knives with stag handle scales which are a permanent part of Solingen's pocket knife production since the 1880s. Even today they are still seen as a typical German product in other countries. The knives usually have a back lock with a trigger protruding from the handle back.

Additional functional parts, such as saw, skinner, gut hook, corkscrew, or bottle opener complement the main blade. Such knives are still very popular among hunters and are offered by the Solingen companies Diefenthal, Hubertus, Linder, and Puma in many versions. The smaller versions of this knife type with one or two blades also look very well as fine gentleman's folders.

The American Way of Knife

In contrast to France and Italy no regional knife shapes developed in the United States—apart from a few exceptions. Nevertheless, classic American pocket knives do show a multitude of different shapes, which is confusing for ordinary people. Some knife patterns were already created in the nineteenth century or even earlier, others developed during the first half of the twentieth century. Since the end of World War II at the latest, American knife catalogs document a relatively stable canon of pocket knife patterns, independent of producers. The names for patterns may vary slightly and sometimes companies offer individual configurations, but there is a fixed portfolio on which manufacturers still build today—not only in the US. German companies such as Böker, Robert Klaas, and Friedrich Olbertz also take these standard patterns as guidelines.

New types that were created after 1945, were mostly limited to the individual company that first offered them. A prominent example is the RussLock of Case, which was introduced in 2000, and received the number "1953" to honor the company's founder Russ Case—it was the year of his death. It was designed by Tom Hart, chief designer of Case for many years. He also designed the CopperLock. Hart developed the RussLock not long before his own death in 1999. Today it is one of Case's most popular patterns.

The multitude of American pocket knife types on the one hand is caused by the configuration of the knives—especially of the blade shapes—which were targeted for special groups of people. Some patterns, such as the cattle or stockman knives, are based on agriculture, others are especially meant for hunting. On the other hand, competitive pressure urged the manufacturers to offer a stream of new patterns or variations of well-known models to distinguish themselves from their competitors.

The construction of traditional American pocket knives follows the sandwich principle. The handle scales and bolsters are mounted on brass liners. Between the liners, for knives with one blade, there is the back spring; knives with more than one blade have two or more springs which—depending on the model—can be separated by additional liners between them. Not every blade necessarily has its own back spring; smaller blades often share one spring. The complete construction is riveted.

In accordance with a common categorization, the American patterns are roughly divided into the three groups "jack knives," "pen knives," and "multi-blade knives." In the first category belong robust utility knives with one or two blades. Usually the blades are attached at the same end of the handle, but there are also patterns such as the two-blade sunfish with the blades on both ends of the handle. The second group encompasses pocket knives of small format with very different handle shapes and blade combinations. Small quill knives with one or two blades belong to this group as well as handy congress knives with four blades. To the third category belong all those pocket knives which have additional tools such as a thorn, can opener, bottle opener, or corkscrew. Many exceptions and special shapes make the unambiguous assignment of a specific pocket knife into one of these categories difficult.

POPULAR TYPES

By and by some of the patterns achieved catchy names, whose origins have been lost in the fog of history. For the determination of a specific pocket knife pattern, the combination of several parameters is decisive: from the length and shape of the handle, the number, size, and order of the blades, up to the shapes of bolsters and blades. A thorough discussion of a single pocket knife pattern with all its historic and producer-specific characteristics could easily fill an entire book. Here, only some of the most interesting and most popular models will be introduced.

One classic that is in the portfolio of every company is the stockman, which in its typical layout has a slightly curved handle and an ensemble of three blades. The main blade is usually a clip point blade, the second a small spey blade, and the third one a sheepsfoot or a pen blade. Sometimes the third tool can also be a thorn.

Case produces the stockman in three sizes, from the Small Stockman with a handle length of 2.75 inches (seven centimeters), the Medium Stockman with a handle length between 3.25 and 3.5 inches (8.3/8.9 centimeters), up to the Large

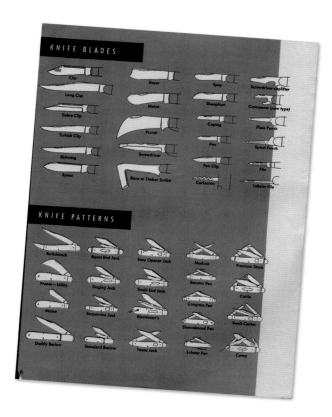

▶ **PAGE FROM A CAMILLUS CATALOG OF 1945:** the different blade shapes are introduced with their popular names.

Stockman with a handle length of 4.25 inches (10.8 centimeters).

Another pattern also produced in several sizes is the Texas toothpick, which presents itself as an especially slim knife with a narrow blade and an inwards-curved handle end. The trapper model is also very popular. Normally it is provided with a combination of long clip point and long spey blade. Besides a large-format model with a handle length of 4 inches (10.2 centimeters) there are also smaller versions. The handle has a more or less pronounced protrusion in the center ("swell-

▶ **NO USUAL STOCKMAN:** the Humpback variant of the "Pocket Worm" series by Case has a humpback-like bulge on the handle's back. In addition, the handle received a special polish so it feels as if it had been worn in the trouser pocket for years.

▶ **FROM GERMAN PRODUCTION (FROM LEFT TO RIGHT):** Stockman of the brand "Jim Bowie" with stag handle scales (made by Friedrich Olbertz), small Stockman by Friedrich Olbertz (own brand) with dark bone scales, and a Mini-Stockman of the brand "Hen & Rooster" (produced by Robert Klaas) with handle scales of bones dyed blue.

center") and is usually provided with bolsters at both ends. The canoe has an especially distinct shape whose symmetrical handle silhouette is similar to that of a canoe, which becomes all the more pronounced due to the upwards-pointing bolsters.

The sunfish is of almost monstrous size. It is also known under the name "elephant's toenail" and many others. It is the biggest among the American pocket knives and is especially striking because of its broad spear point blade. Sometimes the sunfish has a second, smaller blade of the same kind on the opposite handle end.

▸ **POPULAR AMONG COLLECTORS AND USERS:** the Canoe is provided with two spear point blades.

▸ **TWO REPRESENTATIVES OF THE SPECIES SUNFISH:** the knife with the yellow bone scales was produced by Friedrich Olbertz, the other one is a specimen of Great Eastern Cutlery.

▶ **UNUSUAL MATERIAL:** instead of nickel silver, the bolsters of this Barlow knife from Ka-Bar's "Dog's Head" series are made of copper.

▶ **AN AMERICAN CLASSIC:** this Trapper by Case is, typical for the model, provided with two blades in clip point and spey format.

The congress pattern is a very elegant pocket knife, usually provided with four blades. The characteristic features of this pattern are the curved handle and the square bolsters. A model designed in Sheffield that became a legend in the United States is the Barlow knife, which still belongs to the most popular pocket knives. The largest versions of this knife type are marketed under the name Grand Daddy Barlow.

Whoever prefers small-format gentleman's folders ought to search the Case product assortment for the mini-versions of trapper and copperhead or glance at the patterns peanut, baby butterbean, and Eisenhower with a handle length of about three inches (7.6 centimeters). From time to time, Great Eastern Cutlery also produces very handy pocket knives such as the fancy Watch Pocket Sunfish or the classic pen knives of the Esquire series.

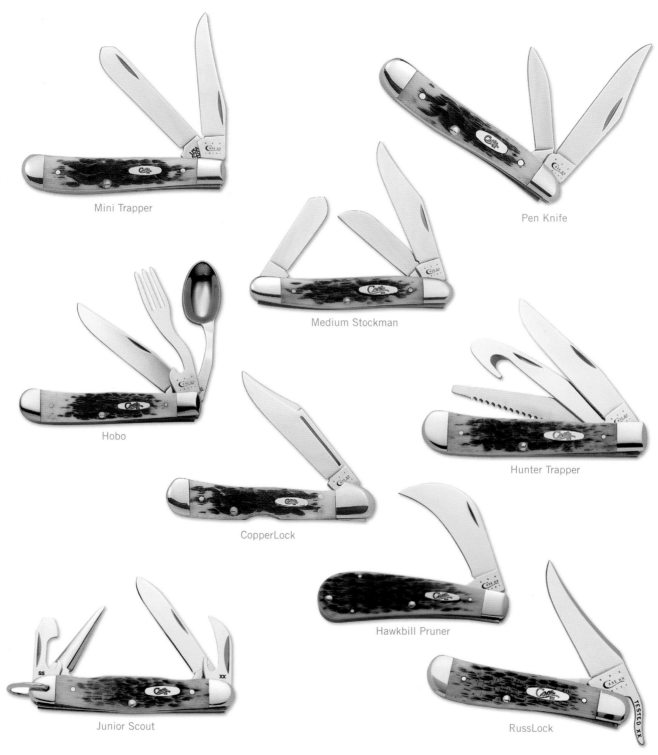

Mini Trapper

Pen Knife

Medium Stockman

Hobo

CopperLock

Hunter Trapper

Hawkbill Pruner

Junior Scout

RussLock

▶ **NINE PATTERNS FROM THE "AMBER BONE" FAMILY BY CASE:** this selection belongs to the
permanent availability program and includes some of the most popular models.

NUMBERING SYSTEMS

Many producers of traditional American pocket knives in the past developed a sophisticated system of abbreviations to mark pattern, configuration, and year of production on the ricasso. Mostly, this is a combination of numbers and letters. Today only Case and Great Eastern Cutlery still use this kind of coding. All abbreviations ever used in the past are decoded on the websites of both companies so even older knives can be identified quickly by means of their help.

Instead of stamping the year of production onto the ricasso, since 2000, Case has used a system of symbols of five crosses and five dots which are each valid for a decennium. The photo depicts the mark for the year 2010: the crosses and dots are still all there. In the years thereafter, first a dot vanishes per year, after that a cross has to go, until only a single cross is left in 2019. After this time, Case will have to come up with a new scheme.

The numbering system of Case is described here by means of an example. On the ricasso, between the land of origin and the steel type "SS" (surgical steel) there is a six-digit number that is best read from back to front. The last four digits "0098" stand for the "pattern number." In this case they stand for the pattern Large Texas Toothpick (in other cases the pattern number can have two or three digits only). The "1" indicates the number of blades and the leading "6" states the handle material to be bone.

Great Eastern Cutlery uses a number consisting of several digits to code the pocket knife pattern as well as its year of production. The two leading digits create the pattern number. The "46" stands for the pattern sunfish or elephant toenail, which is called Whaler in GEC nomenclature. The next digit informs us about the shape of the main blade where "2" is the abbreviation of a spear point blade. The following "2" stands for the number of blades and the last two digits give 2011 as the year of production.

CHAPTER 5

TRADITIONAL KNIVES

Preservation of the Proven

Classic of the First Hour

Because of its long tradition, the cutlery industry has a vast arsenal of names and expressions that are not easily understood by the modern customer. You don't necessarily need the professional jargon of Solingen's dialect: even the expression "*Fahrtenmesser*" (literally: travel knife) does not evoke much of an association for a buyer who is used to the English expression "outdoors knife." Thus the following question may not be so much besides the point: what does a sports knife have to do with sports?

As so often, a look into the time-honored dictionary of the brothers Grimm is helpful. It states about the German word "Sport": "An English word which means the joys of the fields, hunting, racing duels, swimming, and other such pleasurable activities done according to determined rules." This entry reads like the description of any of the most popular leisure time activities of the nineteenth century. But the word "*Freizeit*," German for "free time," is first mentioned in a German dictionary in 1865; in the renowned Duden it was not even mentioned prior to 1929.

When Heinrich Böker, together with Herman Heuser, founded the company Heinr. Böker & Co. in 1869, a word such as "*Freizeitmesser*" ("leisure time knife") would have been too courageous for the creation of a new word. But de facto the *Sportmesser* (sports knife) is a knife for spare time—in contrast, for example, to the army knife, although one use doesn't necessarily exclude another, such as is proven by the Swiss Army Knife for which the expression "*Schweizer Offiziers- und Sportmesser*" ("Swiss officer's and sports knife") was trademarked in 1897.

The Böker sports knife exists since the founding year, 1869. In the course of its history it was cautiously modernized several times. For example, the knife received a bottle opener after the crown cap had conquered the beverage industry. The sports knife was also an export hit on the American market—only interrupted by both world wars. Nothing of the layout has been changed during the past two decades: two blades, a can- and bottle opener can be folded out of the handle; cork screw and awl are placed in the handle's back. Only the handle material is changed from time to time. The scales of oak from the Bergisches Land are an homage to the region of origin.

SPECIFICATIONS

OVERALL LENGTH:	155 mm
BLADE LENGTH:	65 mm
BLADE THICKNESS:	2 mm
WEIGHT:	98 g
HANDLE MATERIAL:	oak
BLADE STEEL:	1.4034
LOCKING MECHANISM:	none
WHERE PRODUCED:	Germany
WEBSITE:	www.boker.de

▸ **MULTIFUNCTIONAL TOOL WITH SIX PARTS:** the Sports Knife has belonged to Böker's model pallete since its founding in 1869. Safety chain and leather pouch round off the configuration.

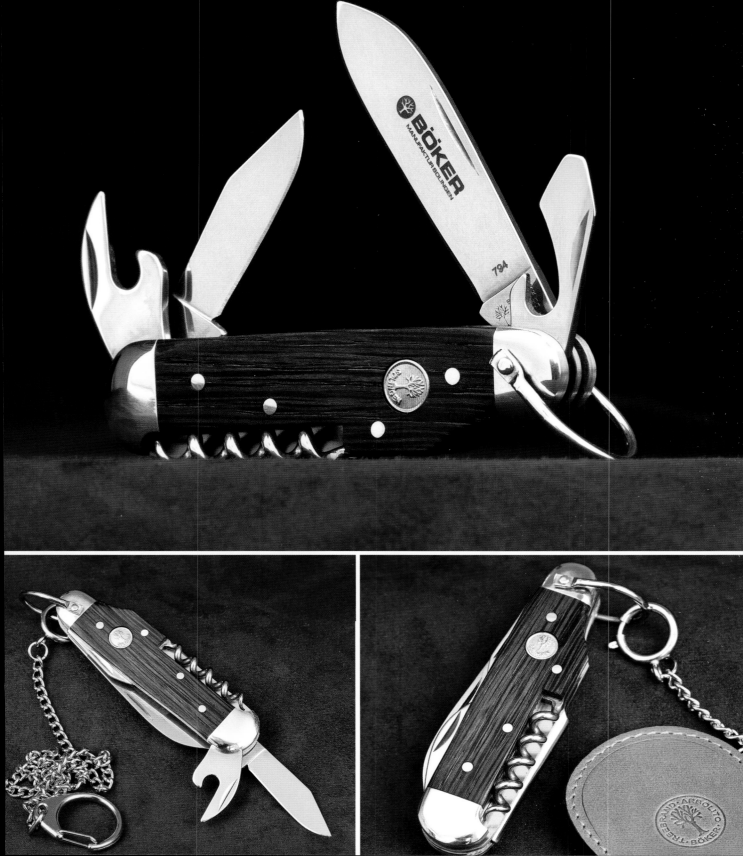

Handmade Since 1890

Hartkopf was a widespread family name in Solingen. Among the ones carrying this name were dubious figures such as the money forger Daniel Hartkopf, who was searched for by warrant for arrest in 1828. But there were also honorable men like the hobby poet Rudolf Hartkopf, who wrote the text to the regional hymn, the *"Bergisches Heimatlied."* This song, first sung by the Solinger Sängerbund on October 30, 1892, praises the native landscape and the art of forging ("the blazing forge, the whirling hammers") and culminates in a romanticization of the empire ready for war, which was typical for the Wilhelmian era of Germany: "when the fatherland calls, when the martial wind roars, courageously the Bergische fist rises up to the conflict."

In those patriotic times, in the year 1890, the pocket knife manufactory Friedrich Hartkopf was founded in Solingen. The year of the company's foundation also marks a new political switch point for Germany. In March 1890, almost two years after he became emperor, young Wilhelm II dismissed the senior imperial chancellor Otto von Bismarck. A British satirical magazine commented on this decision with the famous cartoon "Dropping the Pilot."

The *"Reider"* of pen knives Friedrich Wilhelm Hartkopf—a *"Reider"* was the person who assembled all the parts of a pocket knife—and his newly founded company were successful due to the flourishing overseas trade. New production facilities were bought and the business in Europe expanded. Nevertheless, the company had to endure some setbacks during its history of more than a hundred years. It is all the more pleasing that the company is still owned by the family.

Today Friedrich Hartkopf still produces fine pocket knives such as the model presented here, which has a blade and a combo tool consisting of a bottle opener and a slotted screwdriver. The stainless, random-pattern damascus of Markus Balbach with one hundred layers lifts the knife far above the average of its kind.

By the way, the name Hartkopf shows up confusingly often in the cutlery industry. The well-known reference book *The Sword and Knife Makers of Germany 1850–2000* lists even a dozen companies in Solingen that either once had this name or still have it, among them die forgers and producers of cutlery, scissors, and knives.

SPECIFICATIONS

OVERALL LENGTH:	175 mm
BLADE LENGTH:	75 mm
BLADE THICKNESS:	2 mm
WEIGHT:	66 g
HANDLE MATERIAL:	olive wood
BLADE STEEL:	damascus
LOCKING MECHANISM:	none
WHERE PRODUCED:	Germany
WEBSITE:	www.friedrich-hartkopf.de

▶ **PURE UNDERSTATEMENT:** the deceptively simple olive wood scales and nickel silver bolsters on the outside don't reveal the inner values of this pocket knife. The 100-layer damascus steel of Markus Balbach turns even a bottle opener into an eye-catcher.

Rostfrei 100 Lagen

Westphalian Customs

In 1845, a conservative Catholic newspaper published an article with the title *Westphälische Schilderungen aus einer westphälischen Feder* (Westphalian stories written by a Westphalian quill) which resulted in a formidable scandal. In a brilliant style the anonymous author dissects the conventions and customs of the regions Münsterland, Sauerland, and Paderborner Land, all molded by the Catholic religion. The people of Münsterland are described rather positively; the inhabitants of the Sauerland are said to be offish, cunning, and of lax morals. But the people living in the Paderborner Land are especially bad off: people in this area are said to be shabby and to tend towards superstition, the marriages would be "like a real purgatory" for the women, and quite a few inhabitants would fall victim to the "firewater pestilence."

Immediately after the article was published, a storm of protest arose. Somebody apparently tried to trample down the delicate plant of Westphalian identity, which had slowly started to develop in the Prussian province Westphalia across the borders of religious denominations.

Regardless of how widespread alcoholism was among the inhabitants of Paderborn, the "*Westfälisches Adelsmesser*" (Westphalian Aristocratic Knife) arouses the suspicion that matters were hardly different in upper-class circles: in addition to the blade, the pocket knife has three tools (bottle opener, corkscrew, and champagne hook) that all have the purpose of opening bottles with alcoholic content.

The multi-part pocket knife is inspired by a showpiece in the Deutsches Klingenmuseum (German Blade Museum). It is produced manually by the traditional company Hubertus. As a pocket knife for hunting, it has the typical stag scales, but is also a suitable companion for daily use by non-hunters, due to its compact size. The lockable blade is made of stainless 1.4109-steel.

Despite fierce protests, the editorial department of the newspaper never revealed the name of the anonymous author, who was actually female. None other than the famous Annette von Droste-Hülshoff, author of the novel *Die Judenbuche* (*The Jew's Beech*), and the ballad *Der Knabe vom Moor* (*The Boy on the Moor*), penned this portrait of her fellow countrymen. But this secret was only lifted after her death.

SPECIFICATIONS

OVERALL LENGTH:	140 mm
BLADE LENGTH:	59 mm
BLADE THICKNESS:	3 mm
WEIGHT:	95 g
HANDLE MATERIAL:	stag
BLADE STEEL:	1.4109
LOCKING MECHANISM:	lock back
WHERE PRODUCED:	Germany
WEBSITE:	www.hubertus-solingen.com

▶ **PREPARED FOR ALL CIRCUMSTANCES:** regardless of whether it's champagne, wine, or a beer bottle, the Westphalian Aristocratic Knife made by Hubertus has the proper tool. Of course, it is also able to cut.

Cast from the Same Mold

One blade, two brass liners, two handle scales, four nickel silver bolsters, one spring on the front, one for the lock, and a handful of pins—these are the parts of the model Monolith made by Robert Klaas. But only in the hands of an experienced assembler and grinder at the polishing wheel is a knife created that deserves the name Monolith: it is as if cast from a single mold, all traces of work have been removed, transitions between different materials are no longer palpable.

The Monolith stands in the tradition of pocket hunting knives with back lock. But with its flat construction it is much more delicate than the massive Buck 110, which was the stylish role model for this type of knives. In addition, Robert Klaas uses only exclusive materials, such as the depicted maple wood, whose vivid pattern is a visual pleasure.

Robert Klaas is one of the oldest cutlery companies of Solingen. Its origin can be dated back to 1834, when the former scissor maker Peter Daniel Pauls founded a manufactory for pen knives. From the beginning, the company specialized in high-quality multi-part pocket knives which soon were in demand in the United States, too. After Paul's death, his son-in-law Friedrich Robert Klaas took over the management. Under his name the company was entered in the trade register in 1869. The quickly expanding business repeatedly demanded larger premises. In 1908, the imposing brick building was created, which today is still in use for production, storage, shipping, and administration. The building's gable is decorated by the most prominent trademark of the company: two storks. This symbol, registered in 1893, made an international career as "Kissing Cranes"—despite the ornithologically imprecise translation. Later, in the year 1983, Robert Klaas bought the trademark "Hahn und Henne" from the bankrupt company Bertram. In the United States this mark was well received as "Hen & Rooster."

Tradition is still written in capital letters at the company Robert Klaas, although the production volume has been reduced over the course of decades. The good reputation counts—and every single pocket knife leaving the packing department adds to it.

SPECIFICATIONS

OVERALL LENGTH:	195 mm
BLADE LENGTH:	85 mm
BLADE THICKNESS:	2.5 mm
WEIGHT:	124 g
HANDLE MATERIAL:	maple
BLADE STEEL:	440C
LOCKING MECHANISM:	lock back
WHERE PRODUCED:	Germany
WEBSITE:	www.robert-klaas.de

▸ **FLAGSHIP MODEL:** although the Monolith has been a permanent part of the delivery program only since 1997, it nevertheless represents the long-lasting tradition of craftsmanship of the manufactory Robert Klaas, in existence since 1834.

Beyond the Hunting Folklore

The European polecat (German: *Iltis*) is only rarely mentioned in fables—and it doesn't get a good rap. A Slavic story tells that the hens once wanted to elect a king. But on their search for a suitable candidate they started to quarrel. As even a bloody contest between roosters didn't bring up a clear winner, an old, wise rooster suggested making the polecat their king because as a "tremendous lord with strong teeth" he would provide peace and order. The polecat accepted the honorable offer and promised to protect the poultry against enemies.

As soon as it was on the throne, the polecat's appetite for poultry arose. In order to hide its murderous intentions, he ordered three roosters to his throne consecutively and asked each one whether it would smell something. The first one truthfully answered that it smelled an awful stench. The polecat bit off its head for insulting His Majesty. The second rooster, seeing the dead comrade and the blood-covered king, fearfully lied that there was a wonderful smell. The polecat called him a malicious traitor and bit off its head as well. The third rooster, seeing through this game, stated he had the sniffles and couldn't smell anything. Admiring the rooster's cleverness, the polecat spared its life.

The strong smell is created by two glands at the polecat's rear end, which led to calling it "stinker" in hunter's jargon. The European polecat uses it for marking its territory and driving away enemies. Itself being a hunter of small animals, the European polecat is hunted by humans while its domesticated variant, the ferret, is used for hunting rabbits. With that much importance for hunting, it is no surprise that it became an eponym for a small pocket hunting knife of Solingen's company Linder.

Linder looks back on a long history. During the second half of the nineteenth century already, Carl Wilh. Linder was engaged in the production of pocket knives for hunting. The company today is still in the possession of the family. Similar to many other small pocket hunting knives of Puma or Hubertus, the Iltis, too, is socially acceptable and respectable beyond its use for hunting. The small, unobtrusive knife with handle scales of African blackwood is not bulky in your pocket and—contrary to its animal namesake—is welcomed everywhere.

SPECIFICATIONS

OVERALL LENGTH:	172 mm
BLADE LENGTH:	77 mm
BLADE THICKNESS:	2.5 mm
WEIGHT:	88 g
HANDLE MATERIAL:	African blackwood
BLADE STEEL:	1.4110
LOCKING MECHANISM:	lock back
WHERE PRODUCED:	Germany
WEBSITE:	www.linder.de

▸ **NO STINKER:** beyond all hunting folklore, the Iltis is a handy gent's folder that looks good in every situation. The nickel silver bolsters and the dark African blackwood give this pocket knife its dignified appearance.

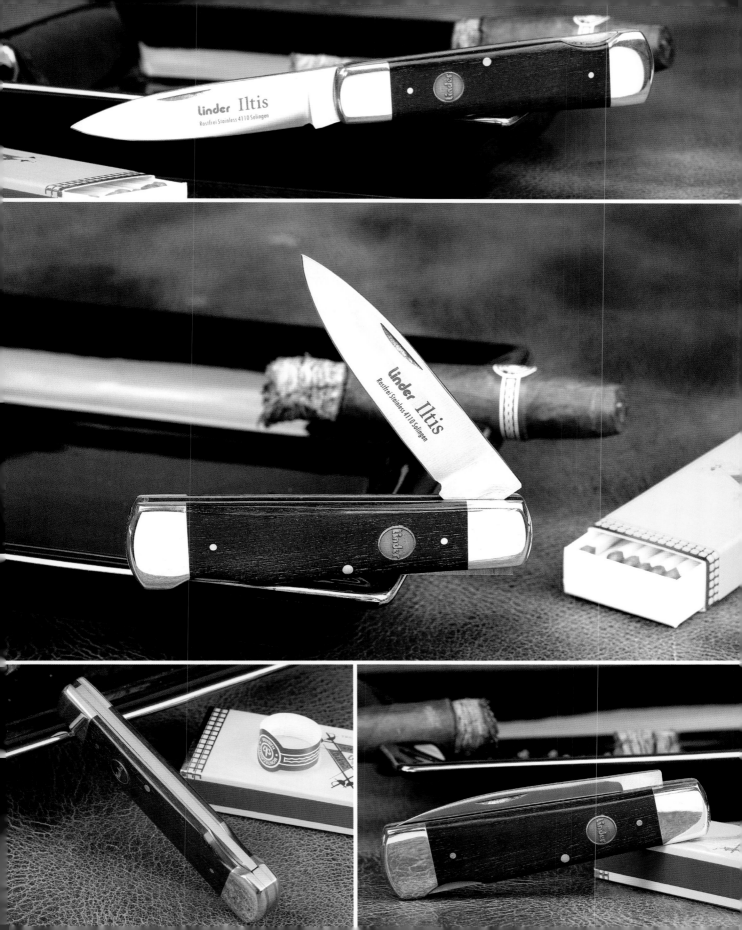

Go West

The history of settlement in the American West features a figure of mythical format: the trapper. He lived in the wilderness, set traps and hunted wild animals, explored unknown territory on his own, and bartered with Native Americans. As a figure with fringed leather jacket and a cap of raccoon fur, the trapper became part of popular iconography.

The status of a national hero was achieved by trapper and pioneer Daniel Boone who in 1775, established the Wilderness Road, following an old path of Native Americans as a first east-west connection across the Appalachian Mountains. For more than five decades it was the only route from the coastal states to Kentucky and further to the Midwest.

When James Fenimore Cooper started writing his famous *Leatherstocking Tales* in the 1820s, Daniel Boone had already become a legend. Episodes from Boone's biography served Cooper as a model for his figure, the trapper Natty Bumppo, who is glorified as a supernatural demigod in an apotheosizing scene of the novel *The Prairie*. At the same time the book is a nostalgic swan song to the untamed wilderness of the North American continent.

Since Cooper's time the trapper belongs to the standard personnel of Wild West adventure novels. Karl May's universe of stories is unthinkable without the noble "*Westmänner*" (men of the west). The later Karl May movies as well as the film adaptation of the *Leatherstocking Tales* with German actor Hellmut Lange as the main character made this type popular and created a cliché.

When the pocket knife pattern named "trapper" first appeared, the fur trade in the United States had long passed its zenith. In American knife catalogs the trapper popped up first in the mid-1920s. But a lot supports the idea that the trapper evolved from a precursor pattern with similar shape and blade layout. The classic trapper pocket knife has two blades of equal length, a clip point and a spey blade. The long version of the spey blade—called "*Kastrierkniep*" in Solingen's dialect—is typical for the trapper pattern.

Friedrich Olbertz produces the trapper depicted here under the label "Bulldog Brand" mainly for the US market, where it is very popular as a utility and collector's knife.

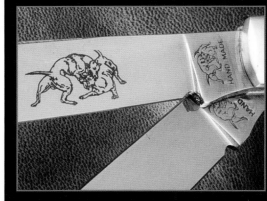

SPECIFICATIONS

OVERALL LENGTH:	187 mm
BLADE LENGTH:	83 mm
BLADE THICKNESS:	2 mm
WEIGHT:	72 g
HANDLE MATERIAL:	oak
BLADE STEEL:	C75
LOCKING MECHANISM:	none
WHERE PRODUCED:	Germany
WEBSITE:	www.pocketknives.de

▶ **MADE FOR THE US MARKET:** the pocket knives of the series "Bulldog Brand," made by Friedrich Olbertz in Solingen, are rare in Germany. They are all the more popular among American collectors.

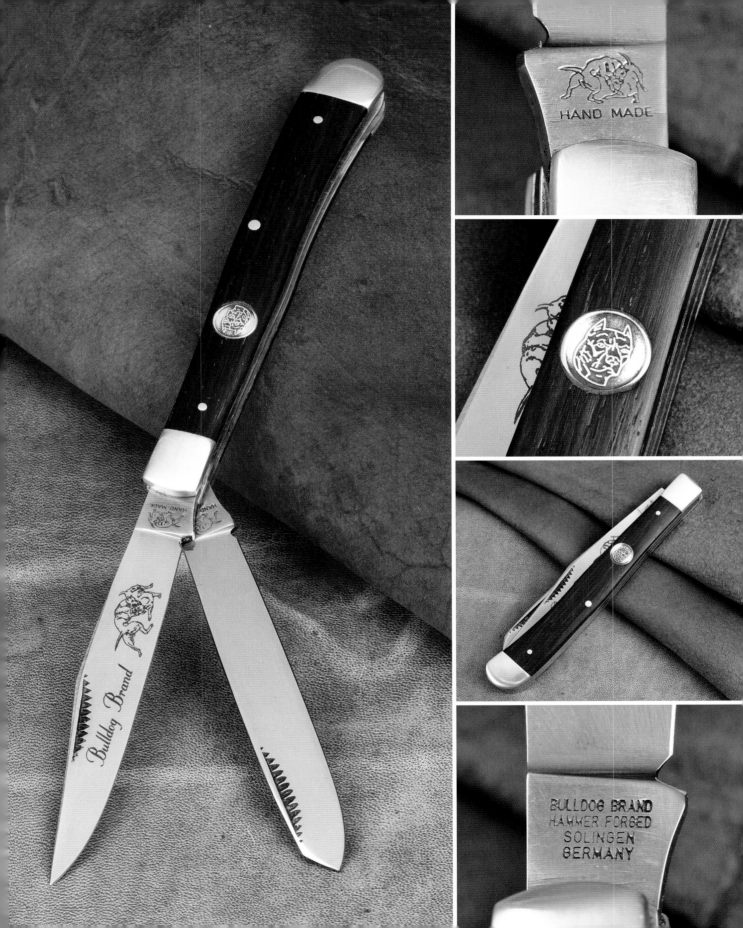

HAND MADE

Bulldog Brand

BULLDOG BRAND
HAMMER FORGED
SOLINGEN
GERMANY

Beloved Poultry

For some strange-sounding brand names surprisingly simple explanations often exist. The brand "Hahn und Henne" is a good example for this: before Carl Bertram turned to fine pen- and pocket knives in 1864, he raised poultry. As "Hen & Rooster" the brand also succeeded in the United States.

Maybe Frank Buster, called Cuz, was a fan of cockfights, because in 1975, he founded the Fight'n Rooster Cutlery Company in Lebanon, Tennessee, which never had production capacities of its own. On the search for a suitable factory for producing his designs of traditional American pocket knives, Cuz struck paydirt in Solingen in the same year. The factory Friedrich Olbertz, back then still headed by Kurt Gronauer, impressed him so much that Cuz from then on produced all his knives there and imported them into the United States. Quickly, his fellow countrymen discovered the exquisite pocket knives of the brand Fight'n Rooster, which are still desired collector's knives. Today the American-German cooperation is continued by the sons Sterling Buster and Achim Gronauer.

The Cattle Knife, produced by Friedrich Olbertz under the brand Fight'n Rooster, is based on a long-serving pattern that can be traced back to around 1870. In those times nobody even thought about collecting pocket knives; the cattle knife was a tool for farmers and is seen as a precursor to the stockman pattern. The symmetrical handle shape, which is rounded at the ends, is typical for this pattern. The knives are usually provided with three, sometimes four blades, but the blade shapes vary considerably. Friedrich Olbertz presents the knife with an ensemble of clip point and sheepsfoot blades combined with a thorn. All three tools are provided with a ninety-degree stop. The dyed bone scales are flanked without any gap by polished bolsters of nickel silver.

As a producer, Friedrich Olbertz doesn't show up on the knives destined for the US market. Only the place of production, Solingen, can be read on the ricasso. Nevertheless, the circles of collectors very well know who they have to thank for the wonderful pocket knives.

SPECIFICATIONS

OVERALL LENGTH:	160 mm
BLADE LENGTH:	70 mm
BLADE THICKNESS:	2.6 mm
WEIGHT:	94 g
HANDLE MATERIAL:	bone
BLADE STEEL:	C75
LOCKING MECHANISM:	none
WHERE PRODUCED:	Germany
WEBSITE:	www.pocketknives.de

▸ **GERMAN-AMERICAN FRIENDSHIP:** since 1975, Friedrich Olbertz in Solingen has been providing the American trade company Fight'n Rooster Cutlery Company with high-quality pocket knives such as this three-part Cattle Knife.

What Is Left of Wilhelm Two

Many US soldiers returning to their homeland after World War II brought a useful souvenir from Germany with them: the "black cat knife." This was what they called the knife because a jumping cat was engraved into the black metal handle. The knife still looks the same as it did even decades earlier.

But the official name of the knife is Mercator, which is a sophisticated wordplay of the inventor Heinrich Kaufmann, who simply translated his family name into Latin. The company Heinrich Kaufmann & Söhne India-Werke, founded in Solingen in 1856, exported cutlery of all kinds to Asia in large quantities. But on the regional market his Mercator knife was especially successful. It is said to have already been invented in 1867, four years prior to the foundation of the German empire, to which it was connected inseparably later on and the lifetime of which it surpassed by far. The success of this knife is not the least based on its simple and almost indestructible construction: the handle consists of a folded box of sheet steel riveted to the blade and the components of the back lock.

In the empire of "Willem Zwo" the Mercator achieved great popularity among civilians as well as soldiers. Thus, in looking back, the Wilhelmian all-purpose knife later received the name "*Kaiser-Wilhelm-Messer*" ("Emperor Wilhelm Knife"). Whether the emperor ever used the knife himself is not known. But we know that Wilhelm II tended to ribald jokes and sometimes cut the suspenders of his high-ranking military officers with a pocket knife during the morning exercises.

Kaufmann later on placed a variant with four parts on the market. Besides the blade it had a corkscrew, can opener, and an awl. In 1995, the company was liquidated; the production of the Mercator went over to the company Otter-Messer in Solingen, which still produces the internationally popular pocket knife with hardly any changes. The version with several parts is also available again.

What about the strange abbreviation "K55K"? The first "K" stands for "Kaufmann," the mirror-inverted second "K" for "*Katze*" (the German word for "cat"). The "55" is derived from the house number in the street of Solingen where once were the headquarters of the India Werke.

SPECIFICATIONS

OVERALL LENGTH:	200 mm
BLADE LENGTH:	90 mm
BLADE THICKNESS:	3 mm
WEIGHT:	74 g
HANDLE MATERIAL:	sheet steel
BLADE STEEL:	C75
LOCKING MECHANISM:	lock back
WHERE PRODUCED:	Germany
WEBSITE:	www.otter-messer.de

▸ **INDESTRUCTIBLE:** the Mercator Knife is a German success story. When it was invented, the later Emperor Wilhelm II was just eight years old. But today it is still linked to the emperor's name.

Praise of the Staghorn

Whoever grew up with Karl May movies probably became acquainted with a Puma knife without even being aware of it. In the movie *Der Schatz im Silbersee*, released in West Germany in 1962 (in the United States as *The Treasure of the Silver Lake* in 1965), and repeatedly shown on TV starting 1974, Lex Barker playing Old Shatterhand fights his way through the Wild West by means of a knife produced by Solingen's long-established company Puma. It was the model White Hunter, which had already been designed in 1956, but only received its cult status through this movie.

An air of Wild West was around this brand from the beginning, since the cougar or mountain lion only lives in the Americas. In contrast, the origin of the company lies in the Bergisches Land and its history goes back to the time when only water power was driving the grinding stones in the workshops along the river Wupper. In 1769, Johann Wilhelm Lauterjung had his brand symbol registered in the roll of Solingen's knifemakers. The consistent orientation of its product range towards the areas hunting, sports, and outdoors during the 1950s, still characterizes the premium range of Puma products. With the introduction of the series "Puma IP" (produced in Spain) and "Puma TEC" (produced in China) the product palette was broadened to include low-cost utility knives in a modern style.

The Pocket Hunting Knife I is made in Solingen and has—how could it be otherwise—stag handle scales. The material is warm, non-slip, and a traditional part of hunting folklore. The bolsters and a hexagonal platelet for engravings made of nickel silver round off the classic appearance. But because of its compact dimensions, the pocket knife is also well-suited as an everyday carry in the urban environment.

The practical small hunting knives with stag handle scales, which are still offered by companies such as Puma, Hartkopf, Hubertus, and Linder (all from Solingen), defy the overall trend towards stylish shapes and modern synthetic handle materials. Young people may sneer at them as old-fashioned grandpa pocket knives. But whoever grew up with The Treasure of the Silver Lake knows that stag can also be "cool." After all, Old Shatterhand's knife was provided with this material.

SPECIFICATIONS

OVERALL LENGTH:	170 mm
BLADE LENGTH:	76 mm
BLADE THICKNESS:	3 mm
WEIGHT:	92 g
HANDLE MATERIAL:	stag
BLADE STEEL:	1.4110
LOCKING MECHANISM:	back lock
WHERE PRODUCED:	Germany
WEBSITE:	www.pumaknives.de

▸ **UNDER THE SIGN OF THE MOUNTAIN LION:** the Pocket Hunting Knife I is a typical Puma knife. The characteristic scales of stag, of course, can't be absent. The trigger protruding from the handle back can even be used easily with gloves.

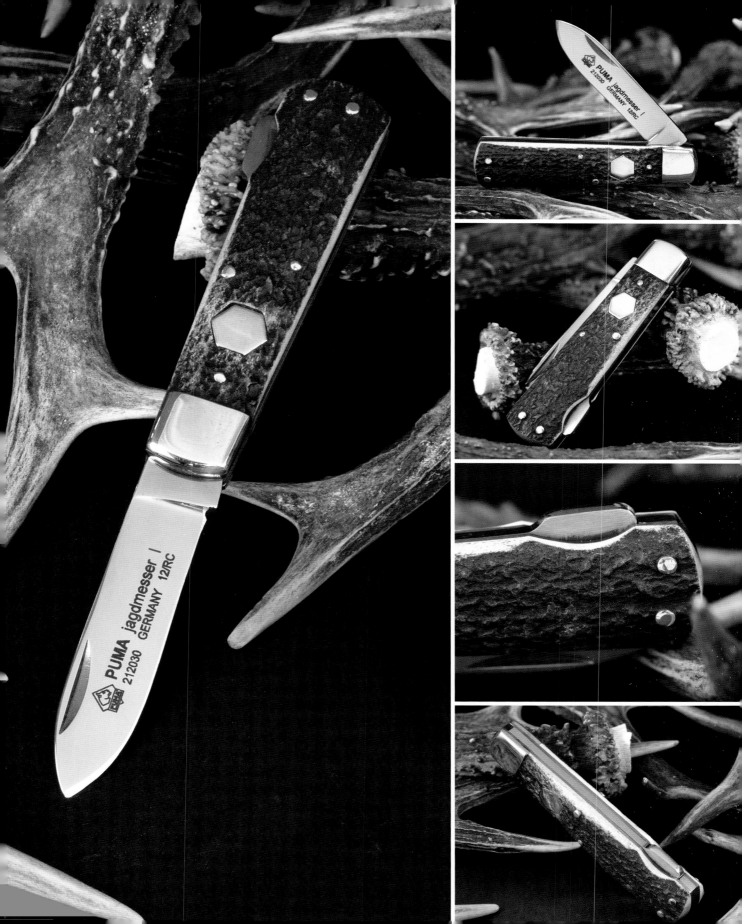

Success Within the Niche

It doesn't always have to be Thiers. In the village Viscomtat, a bit apart from France's knife metropolis, Renaud Aubry has a small knife atelier. The handmade knives are distributed under the brand name "Artisan Coutelier" which, compared to the grand names from Thiers still has the status of an insider's tip.

Although Aubry also produces the popular Laguiole knives, his specialty is a small-format slipjoint pocket knife based on an old pattern. The Navette is known in France since the nineteenth century. It owes its name to the handle shape, which is rounded at the ends and thus looks like a weaver's shuttle (in French "la navette"). But the knife didn't originate in the famous silk weaving mills of Lyon where in 1831, there was a big riot because the prices for the purchase of silk products, which had fallen for years, had led small family businesses into poverty and debt. A fine pocket knife at this time would have been an unaffordable luxury item.

Renaud Aubry prefers the simple variant with one blade, although the Navette traditionally could be equipped with additional tools such as cork screw, bottle opener, or can opener. The model shown here is of high-quality workmanship. The handle scales are made of bark mammoth ivory, the delicate floral decorations on the spring were driven into the material with a chasing punch ("ciselage au burin")—an attractive alternative compared to the usual filework. Layers of black fiber between scales and liners of stainless steel set another optical accent.

Whoever likes it simpler can configure his/her own Navette on the website of "Artisan Coutelier" according to their personal wishes. Since the Navette, in contrast to other French regional knives, is only produced by very few companies, Renaud Aubry has opened up an exclusive market niche by means of this knife. Since October 2013, he has been offering a distinctly larger model in addition. Initially it was supposed to be named "La Grande Navette" but eventually received the apt name "Le Vicomte" due to its imposing character.

SPECIFICATIONS

OVERALL LENGTH:	166 mm
BLADE LENGTH:	74 mm
BLADE THICKNESS:	2.5 mm
WEIGHT:	60 g
HANDLE MATERIAL:	mammoth ivory
BLADE STEEL:	12C27
LOCKING MECHANISM:	none
WHERE PRODUCED:	France
WEBSITE:	www.artisancoutelier.com

▸ **ARTISTIC LITTLE GEM OF FRANCE:** in the version with handle scales of mammoth ivory the Navette looks especially precious. The name hints at the similarity of the handle to a weaver's shuttle, which belongs to the equipment of traditional hand looms.

The Lovely Garonne

In early December 1801, the German poet Friedrich Hölderlin started a marathon walk from Nürtingen to Bordeaux. He walked through the Black Forest to Strasbourg and from there over the snowy mountains of the Auvergne to Lyon and on to Bordeaux, where he arrived at the end of January 1802, to take a job as tutor. But as soon as the end of June he appeared back in Stuttgart, bedraggled and bewildered. Hölderlin's winter walk is still mysterious today.

His stay in Bordeaux he later poetically converted into the well-known hymn "*Andenken*" ("Remembrance"), which is cause for all kinds of deep speculations. But first and foremost it expresses the memory of the landscape around Bordeaux in beautiful images. The poem envisions the "lovely Garonne" and the "gardens of Bordeaux" with nostalgic longing, it speaks of the "hill sides of grapes" whence "the Dordogne descends toward the majestic Garonne" to flow into the Atlantic "as one wide sea." It is this landscape in the southwest of France that is home to the pocket knife Garonnais, named after the river. But as mysterious as Hölderlin's trip is the history of this pocket knife.

The Garonnais is a stable all-purpose knife with spear point blade which has a certain similarity to the Pradel. The knife forge Au Sabot offers the Garonnais in a simple version with handle scales of ebony. The tight back spring has no decorations; the only decorative element is the small escutcheon with the embossed Occitan cross (also called Toulouse cross) pointing to the roots of the knife within the region. The Occitan language is spoken in the southern third of France but also in the Val d'Aran in the Catalan Pyrenees, the area of the Garonne's headwaters.

The wooden shoe decorating the blade ("le sabot" in French) was registered as a brand logo by Etienne Fontenille in 1870. The company Au Sabot is owned by the family Sauzedde since 1973. When buying one of the traditional knives produced by Au Sabot you have to be aware that the products are low-cost and simple. Thus you should not expect the same production quality as with a far more expensive knife made by one of the high-end companies of Thiers.

SPECIFICATIONS

OVERALL LENGTH:	190 mm
BLADE LENGTH:	85 mm
BLADE THICKNESS:	3 mm
WEIGHT:	90 g
HANDLE MATERIAL:	ebony
BLADE STEEL:	12C27
LOCKING MECHANISM:	none
WHERE PRODUCED:	France
WEBSITE:	www.ausabot.com

▸ **NAMED AFTER A RIVER:** the roots of the Garonnais lie in southwestern France where the "lovely Garonne" (Hölderlin), originating in the Spanish Pyrenees, combines with the Dordogne near Bordeaux.

A Friend for a Lifetime

Le Compagnon: this name is perhaps the prettiest and best-sounding name ever given to a pocket knife. Because with respect to the meaning of the word, a compagnon is somebody with whom you share your bread. The word is derived from the Latin "*cum pane*" which is also in the German word "*Kumpan*" and the English "companion." A knife bearing this name should thus be a constant companion, a friend for a lifetime. That such a knife originates in France is no wonder. Who, if not the French, know best that you always should have a knife around for the small, social in-between meals with baguette, saucisson (sausage) and cheese?

The Compagnon of Chambriard is a pocket knife in "Le Thiers" style. Indeed, it is one of the first of its kind, because when it was launched in 1998, the creation of the "Confrérie du Couteau de Thiers" had been just a few years before. This society of enthusiasts had decided to set a monument to the city of Thiers in the form of a knife. The prototype was introduced to the public in 1994.

Knifesmith Dominique Chambriard belonged to the founding members of the society. His family has been working in the field of cutlery since 1918. Dominique and his brother Philippe have a large retail store in Thiers with knives of more than 160 producers. In addition, they run a small manufactory for pocket knives that excel in their outstanding quality of craftsmanship.

The version of the Compagnon introduced here has handle scales of juniper with a peppery scent. The knife is of solid construction with liners and bolsters of stainless steel; the back spring is stylishly decorated with guilloche. The "Le Thiers" logo is embossed into the blade of 13C26 steel. Only those knives which succeed in a strict testing process are allowed to wear this logo. Its compact form—a "T" with dot—is punched into the spring's head.

After the Compagnon, Chambriard released the models Compact and Trappeur as a smaller and a larger variant. And since a "*casse-croûte*" (snack) without wine is hardly thinkable, the Compagnon is also available with corkscrew. This model has the well-chosen name Le Grand Cru.

SPECIFICATIONS

OVERALL LENGTH:	205 mm
BLADE LENGTH:	95 mm
BLADE THICKNESS:	3 mm
WEIGHT:	88 g
HANDLE MATERIAL:	juniper
BLADE STEEL:	13C26
LOCKING MECHANISM:	none
WHERE PRODUCED:	France
WEBSITE:	www.coutellerie-chambriard.com

▸ **TASTEFUL LIFESTYLE:** for the snack in between, in French called "casse-croûte," the Compagnon by Chambriard is the ideal choice. This knife has been the figurehead of the manufactory from Thiers since 1998.

The Demon and the Knife

The year 1929 marks the birth of some prominent cartoon and comic figures that are still present in the collective memory. In the United States, newspaper readers for the first time followed the adventures of space hero Buck Rogers, the brawling sailor Popeye had his debut as a cartoon hero, and the untamed nature-boy Tarzan showed up in comic strips for the first time. In Belgium, Tintin and Milou saw first light, and in France a strange figure showed up, who could have originated in the jungle world of Tarzan and might even have had what it takes to become an adversary of Buck Rogers.

This figure wasn't released as a print, but on a knife handle: Gaspard Cognet, a knifesmith of Thiers just had designed a pocket knife meant for the French colonies in Oceania. To give the knife a bit of the local color of the target market, he embossed a demon of this far-away island world onto the handle: duk-duk, a figure that wears leaves as clothing and has a helmet-like, slender, conical mask. This mysterious spirit appears regularly in the night of the new moon to receive food offerings by humans. At the same time it is a type of South Seas big brother who knows all sins of the humans and punishes them with whacks or even with death.

But is the figure discovered by Cognet in a book a demon at all? Or is it a dancer of the Melanesian duk-duk cult popular on the islands northeast of Australia? Whichever it is: Cognet put the French name "Douk-Douk" underneath the figure and thus unknowingly created a knife legend.

The Douk-Douk is a robust, repair-friendly and low-cost knife made of just six parts. Inside a folded piece of sheet steel two rivets hold a strong spring and a blade of carbon steel in place; a small metal lug serves as an eyelet for the lanyard. Since 1929, nothing has been changed with respect to construction and production. However, the knife was not only exported to the islands of the Pacific but found its largest distribution in the African colonies of France, where it was not always used for peaceful purposes. Today the Douk-Douk is well known around the world.

SPECIFICATIONS

OVERALL LENGTH:	162 mm
BLADE LENGTH:	75 mm
BLADE THICKNESS:	2.5 mm
WEIGHT:	36 g
HANDLE MATERIAL:	sheet steel
BLADE STEEL:	XC75
LOCKING MECHANISM:	none
WHERE PRODUCED:	France
WEBSITE:	www.douk-douk.com

▶ **CULT OBJECT:** the Douk-Douk initially was a simple work knife for use in the French colonies. Its construction is simple, the finish is rustic. The rough charm of the small version with a blade length of 75 mm nevertheless evokes enthusiasm.

Laguiole 2.0

You can quarrel wonderfully about the authenticity of a Laguiole knife. There is the faction stating that only a knife manufactured completely in Laguiole is worthy of carrying that name. But you have to take into account that the production of these famous knives—mostly for capacity reasons—was already increasingly moved to Thiers during the last third of the nineteenth century and that after the end of World War I no significant numbers were produced directly in Laguiole. Only with the foundation of the Forge de Laguiole in 1987, did the local forging and production technologies start to revive. However, there is no genealogical connection between the Forge and the knifesmith families of the nineteenth century.

Thus it is improper to deny the right of producing "authentic" Laguiole knives to the long-established manufactories in Thiers. The decisive criterion for judging a Laguiole should be its quality only.

The company Fontenille Pataud, founded in Thiers in 1929, was a synonym for high-quality table cutlery for decades, but the trend towards dishwasher-safe dishes made it increasingly more difficult to succeed in this market segment. When Gilles Steinberg bought the company in 1994, he resorted to the production of high-quality pocket knives. And he dared to modernize the flagship of French knife tradition. One known annoyance is that the blade edge of a classical Laguiole bangs against the back spring when closing the knife without slowing the blade down. Thus all Laguiole knives by Fontenille Pataud are provided with a blade stop, an additional pin at the handle's inside, which provides a sufficient distance between blade and spring. In addition, some model series—such as the Laguiole of the "Nature" series introduced here—are provided with a back lock.

The production quality of the knives made by Fontenille Pataud is at the highest level—starting with the velvet-smooth blade movement and the gap-free fit of the handle components to the neatly centered blade and the delicately worked guilloche. Gilles Steinberg's name stands for the quality of his knives. Each knife carries the lettering "Gilles."

SPECIFICATIONS

OVERALL LENGTH:	217 mm
BLADE LENGTH:	97 mm
BLADE THICKNESS:	3 mm
WEIGHT:	100 g
HANDLE MATERIAL:	buffalo horn
BLADE STEEL:	12C27
LOCKING MECHANISM:	back lock
WHERE PRODUCED:	France
WEBSITE:	www.fontenille-pataud.com

▸ **CAREFULLY MODERNIZED:** nobody at Fontenille Pataud is a friend of wrongly interpreted nostalgia. All Laguiole models are provided with a blade stop; the knives of the series "Nature" in addition are equipped with a back lock.

Back to the Roots

In the competition for attention of their customers, the producers of Laguiole knives sometimes outperform each other with respect to the configuration of their wares. The trend towards increasingly more exotic handle materials and more elaborately decorated liners and springs is contrasted with the model Ancestral of Laguiole en Aubrac. This model is meant to remind you of the simple original shape of the Laguiole knife as produced between 1830 and 1870. Although the Ancestral is no exact replica of an original knife of this time period—the modern steel 12C27 was used for the blade—it nevertheless gives a good impression of the "ancestral Laguiole."

The first thing to catch one's eye is the straight handle design in contrast to the well-known curved shape, which is the reason why the ancestral Laguiole is also called "Laguiole droit." The blade doesn't have the typical Yatagan-shape yet. And the pins, underlaid with brass rings, hint at the handle construction common in the nineteenth century. In addition, this construction does without the bolsters that are customary today. What may be most astonishing for a modern observer is the flat, unornamented head of the spring. Where is the famous bee? Indeed, the bee first appeared around 1908. It was an innovation of Jules Calmels, the grandchild of Pierre Jean Calmels, the Laguiole's inventor.

The simple construction of the Ancestral may remind one that the Laguiole initially was a simple utility knife not suited as a symbol of status. Only with the refined taste of the citizens of Paris, who noticed the knife with the immigrants from the Auvergne, did a desire for more artsy designs arise.

The manufactory Laguiole en Aubrac resides in the village Espalion, about twenty minutes from Laguiole with a car. Quite often it is forgotten that at this time the family of Pierre Jean Calmels wasn't the only one participating in the production of knives. In Espalion, the coutellierie of the family Salertes was founded in 1874. The family was connected to the families Calmels and Pagès in Laguiole by marriage. Further family businesses were located in Saint-Urcize, Saint-Geniez-d'Olt, and Sévérac-le-Château. Back at that time probably nobody would have hit on the idea to declare Laguiole to be the only legitimate place for the production of this successful model which today we see as the Laguiole knife.

SPECIFICATIONS

OVERALL LENGTH:	210 mm
BLADE LENGTH:	95 mm
BLADE THICKNESS:	3 mm
WEIGHT:	74 g
HANDLE MATERIAL:	olive wood
BLADE STEEL:	12C27
LOCKING MECHANISM:	none
WHERE PRODUCED:	France
WEBSITE:	www.laguiole-en-aubrac.fr

▶ **STRAIGHT AND WITHOUT A BEE:** the Ancestral takes up the original shape of the "Laguiole droit." The original Laguiole had neither the curved handle shape nor the decorated head of the back spring.

Sharp Stuff
from the Périgord

The claim of being the oldest knife of France can be raised by (at least) two candidates: on the one hand there is the Capucin from the Pyrenees supported by its simple construction, on the other hand the pocket knives of Nontron look back on a long history. Probably the question can't be solved definitively.

The beginnings of knife production in the village Nontron, located in the north of the Périgord, date back to medieval times. Similar to the Bergisches Land around Solingen, natural conditions were favorable: iron ore in the area of Nontron had been mined since Gallo-Roman times; an abundant forest supply as well as natural water power kept the charcoal kilns, smelting furnaces, and forges running.

The famous Nontron folder has its origin in the fifteenth century—way before the first Laguiole or Opinel existed. The handle is traditionally turned from regional boxwood considered to be especially hard. As an indeciduous shrub, the common boxwood is also a symbol for eternal life. The handle butt is finished as a "*boule*" (sphere), "*sabot*" (wooden shoe), "*queue de carpe*" (carp tail), or "*double virole*" (double ferrule). The knives are produced in different sizes—down to quaint miniatures.

However, the handle of the Nontron model No.25 presented here is not made of bright boxwood but dark ebony. Thus the usual pyrographic decoration (pokerwork), with the (still mysterious) symbol called "*mouche*" (fly)—a "V" turned upside down with three dots—burnt into the wood, is not executed. In this simple form the knife appears more elegant and less folksy than the classic boxwood Nontron.

The blade is arrested by means of a twistable ferrule (virole) of nickel silver. In contrast to the modern Virobloc system of Opinel, the ferrule blocks the blade only in open position, not when it is closed. Because the Coutellerie Nontronnaise belongs to the Forge de Laguiole since 1992, the same stainless T12-steel used by the Forge for its Laguiole knives is used for this forged and polished blade as well.

SPECIFICATIONS

OVERALL LENGTH:	210 mm
BLADE LENGTH:	90 mm
BLADE THICKNESS:	2 mm
WEIGHT:	50 g
HANDLE MATERIAL:	ebony
BLADE STEEL:	T12
LOCKING MECHANISM:	twistable ferrule
WHERE PRODUCED:	France
WEBSITE:	www.coutellerie-nontronnaise.fr

▸ **STRAIGHT AS A CANDLE:** two ferrules (double virole) of nickel silver frame the ebony handle. The upper ring can be rotated and blocks the open blade—a mechanism created long before Opinel's Virobloc system.

Utopia and Heresy

In Foix, capital of the department Ariège at the foot of the Pyrenees, Olivier Montariol runs the retail store Savignac, which carries the name of the family who owned it in the twentieth century. Its beginnings date back to the year 1754. Adjacent to the showroom is a small workshop in which Olivier Montariol continues the tradition of his predecessors. Here he produces pocket knives with a regional reference to landscape and history of Occitania.

The model L'Ariégois, named after the region, serves as a figurehead. It is a friction folder assuming the ancient shape of the Capucin which was once the knife of the rural population in the South of France. In a specialized book from 1772, it is described as "un couteau à deux clous," a knife with two metal pins: one serves as a blade axis, the other as blade stop. The model Cathare also follows this simple construction. Olivier Montariol offers it in two sizes and with various handle materials. In addition, the customer can choose between carbon steel, stainless 12C27, and damascus. The knife is provided with a leaf-shaped blade and a smoothly curved handle whose width tapers towards the end. In a leather pouch the lightweight knife can be taken along comfortably everywhere.

The name of the folding knife is homage to the times of the Cathars, a time of great hopes which today is almost forgotten. The Cathars— literally "the pure"—turned away from the Roman-Catholic church in the twelfth century. They condemned the pomposity of Catholic dignitaries and wanted to establish a church for the poor. The movement quickly found many followers and spread from the Pyrenees to the river Rhine. But it found its largest reception in Occitania, where powerful nobles sympathized with Catharism. In Rome, the teachings of the Cathars were seen as heresy. And since the French crown had wanted to incorporate Occitania into its territory for a long time already, pope and king bound together and led a gruesome annihilation campaign against the Cathars. In 1244, the last of the Cathars still alive, who had withdrawn to the castle Montségur near Foix, surrendered. They were burned as heretics.

SPECIFICATIONS

OVERALL LENGTH:	100 mm
BLADE LENGTH:	73 mm
BLADE THICKNESS:	2.5 mm
WEIGHT:	36 g
HANDLE MATERIAL:	olive wood
BLADE STEEL:	XC75
LOCKING MECHANISM:	none
WHERE PRODUCED:	France
WEBSITE:	www.couteau-savignac.com

▸ **RICH IN HISTORY:** the Cathare is a friction folder that reminds one of a forgotten period of Medieval Europe. Centuries before Luther, the Catharist movement wanted to reform the church. Rome answered with a crusade and exterminated the heretics.

The Scantiness of the Cantal

The engraving on the ricasso—a crown flanked by the letters "G" and "R"—is the proud sign of Gilles Reynewaeter, who has lead the fortunes of the traditional manufactory Thiers-Issard since 1985. Before that time, the company was owned by the family Thiers.

Founded in 1884, by Pierre Thiers, the company achieved an excellent reputation far beyond the borders of France, especially with their manually forged razors. Pierre Thiers was the offspring of an old family from the city of the same name and was already sent to a razor smith for training at the tender age of ten. In the following years he developed into a master of his trade and opened his own forge. To distinguish himself from other family members working in the same profession, he added the family name of his wife to his own. Today Thiers-Issard still produces premium razors but also other kinds of cutlery, among them Laguiole- and regional knives.

The Aurillac, named after the capital of the Cantal, initially was a knife of farmers and herders of this barren mountain region in the Massif Central, which reached literary fame through the novel *Perfume: The Story of a Murderer* by German author Patrick Süsskind. The summit of the Plomb du Cantal is described there as, "the most remote point within the entire kingdom"; "Even in bright daylight this area was of such desolate inhospitality that the poorest shepherd of the already poor province would not have moved his animals to here." The main figure Jean-Baptiste Grenouille withdrew to the reclusiveness of this mountain for seven years.

Characteristic features of the knife are the sloping line towards the blade tip (Bourbonnais blade shape) and the comfortable curve at the handle's bottom side. The dark-spotted snakewood, of course, is no handle material typical for the region. Since the wood is very hard and not prone to abrasion, it was used for print letters in the past. Thus snakewood in French is also known under the name "*lettre mouchetée*" (speckled letter). But initially regional wood types or horn and calf bone of Salers cattle were used—an ancient race of domestic cattle with red-brown fur and horns shaped like a lyre.

SPECIFICATIONS

OVERALL LENGTH:	178 mm
BLADE LENGTH:	80 mm
BLADE THICKNESS:	2.5 mm
WEIGHT:	62 g
HANDLE MATERIAL:	snakewood
BLADE STEEL:	12C27
LOCKING MECHANISM:	none
WHERE PRODUCED:	France
WEBSITE:	www.thiers-issard.fr

▶ **MORE THAN 100 YEARS OF TRADITIONAL CRAFTSMANSHIP:** the manufactory Thiers-Issard, founded in 1884, is well-known for its excellent razors. In addition, it produces French regional knives such as this pretty Aurillac with snake wood handle scales and lots of guilloche.

The Way of a British Gentleman

In the nineteenth century, in America a Barlow knife was the pride of every boy. How deep this knife is rooted in the American culture is proven by the old traditional *Shady Grove* ("When I was a little boy/I wanted a Barlow knife"), but also by Mark Twain's much-read novel *The Adventures of Tom Sawyer* in which the author eternalized the knife. Scalawag Tom receives it from his cousin as a prize for learning Bible verses by heart: "Mary gave him a brand-new 'Barlow' knife, worth twelve and a half cents; and the convulsion of delight that swept his system shook him to his foundations. True, the knife would not cut anything, but it was a 'sure enough' Barlow, and there was inconceivable grandeur in that."

A twelve-and-a-half-cent Barlow was, even for the conditions in these times—measured by the value of the dollar around 1845, the approximate time of the novel's storyline—a cheap knife. You have to visualize it as a coarsely made pocket knife with no time squandered on polishing the handle or blade.

Tom's knife thus would hardly be comparable to the Barlow knife by Taylor's Eye Witness, which presents itself as a British high-class cutting tool with decorated spring, mirror-polished blade, and exquisite wood. Only with respect to their contour could both knives be assigned to the same type. The drop-shaped handle and the long, stretched bolsters are characteristic for the Barlow pattern originating in Sheffield. Probably it was a certain Obadiah Barlow who first produced it around 1670; his grandchild John exported it successfully to America in the nineteenth century. There it was quickly imitated so that it was seen as a typical American folding knife in later years.

The "Eye Witness" brand, registered by John Taylor in Sheffield in 1838, is one of the few that survived the downfall of the English cutlery industry in the twentieth century. Using the still-strong aura of the brand, the company Harrison Fisher & Co, which had bought the brand in 1975, renamed it as Taylor's Eye Witness in 2007. This handmade Barlow is a worthy testimony to Sheffield's pocket knife tradition.

SPECIFICATIONS

OVERALL LENGTH:	155 mm
BLADE LENGTH:	67 mm
BLADE THICKNESS:	2 mm
WEIGHT:	75 g
HANDLE MATERIAL:	ironwood
BLADE STEEL:	420HC
LOCKING MECHANISM:	none
WHERE PRODUCED:	England
WEBSITE:	www.taylors-eye-witness.co.uk

▸ **THE ALL-SEEING EYE:** this symbol, which already appeared in Egyptian mythology, was also used by Carl Schlieper for his brand known as "German Eye." John Taylor was inspired to the "Eye Witness" brand by a verse from William Shakespeare's *Henry IV*.

A Comet of the Toscana

The manufactory ConAz was founded in the mid-1950s, by the brothers Luigi and Enrico Consigli and their friend Marcello Azzini in Scarperia (the company's name is put together from the first letters of both family names). The products offered range from classic Italian regional knives, table and kitchen knives, to small series of elaborately finished collector's knives. By means of the consistently high quality the family business was able to successfully place the brand Consigli on the international market.

In the canon of Italy's traditional pocket knives, the Tre Pianelle ("three plates") belongs to the less well-known models. It has been produced in Scarperia since the nineteenth century. Its name originates from the special blade shape: the blade is ground in such a way as to create three surfaces separated from each other by distinct steps. The spearpoint blade reminds one of a dagger, but the blade's back is not sharpened. On the generously-dimensioned ricasso a stylized comet is engraved underneath two intersecting lines. This special symbol has its origin in a statute of 1630, that obligates all knifesmiths of Scarperia to mark their products with an individually modified image of a comet. Consigli sees this symbol as a sign of illuminating power and dynamic.

The handle is made from a solid piece of buffalo horn with the recess for blade and spring sawed into it. The completely riveted knife construction doesn't need any liners. The blade is held in position in an absolutely reliable way by means of the tight spring. When closing the knife, a ninety-degree blade stop provides safe handling. But you should not let the blade snap the rest of the way without holding it, because otherwise the blade will hit against the handle's inside. This little nuisance is not bad workmanship but exists due to the historic construction.

The flawless quality of craftsmanship is self-evident for Consigli knives. You could complain about the outdated blade steel, in case you really want to do rough cutting-and whittling jobs with this fine knife—but who wants to do this in earnest?

SPECIFICATIONS

OVERALL LENGTH:	205 mm
BLADE LENGTH:	90 mm
BLADE THICKNESS:	3 mm
WEIGHT:	72 g
HANDLE MATERIAL:	buffalo horn
BLADE STEEL:	420
LOCKING MECHANISM:	none
WHERE PRODUCED:	Italy
WEBSITE:	www.consigliscarperia.it

▸ **TUSCANY FLAIR:** the Tre Pianelle owes its name to the special blade geometry with three distinctly separated surfaces coming together at the blade tip.

The Saladini Syndrome

Since the Renaissance, the Grand Tour belongs to the standard education program for the sons of European aristocracy and, later, of the propertied bourgeoisie. In Italy, due to its rich treasures of art, the city of Florence belonged to the popular stations on the trip—besides Venice, Rome, and Naples.

When Goethe went on his big trip to Italy in 1786, he hardly gave a glance at the capital of the Tuscany: "The desire to get to Rome was so strong, grew so much with every moment that there was no staying, and I was in Florence for no more than three hours." The British author Laurence Sterne, too, twenty years earlier had turned a cold shoulder on art and renaissance architecture of the city. Just the opposite of French author Stendhal: when he visited Florence at the beginning of the nineteenth century, he was overwhelmed by the ever-present cultural impressions so much that he had a nervous breakdown.

Whether the sensory overload from culture really leads to psychosomatic dysfunctions with Florence tourists is wildly debated. Nevertheless, the phenomenon entered the specialist literature as Stendhal syndrome.

The danger of pathological ecstasy also exists when seeing the traditional Italian knives of the small manufactory Saladini located in the historic center of Scarperia. The Fiorentino, the popular knife of Florence, is a classic dating back to models of the eighteenth century which were common throughout Tuscany.

The Fiorentino's handle scales are made of silky-gleaming buffalo horn. A ferrule, engraved by hand and made of silver, is the optical transition to the bulgy blade. The handle end is decorated with a button also made of silver with an engraved flower motif. In contrast to the similar model Zuava, the handle construction of the Florentine doesn't need additional liners, which doesn't weaken stability, but instead keeps the weight down. With about 80 grams, the knife is pleasantly lightweight.

The Grand Tour lost its exclusivity in the nineteenth century. Classical ideals were no longer in demand; Romanticism was now highly popular, and the Romantics had discovered the Middle Ages. Nevertheless, the Fiorentino has defied all fashions until today.

SPECIFICATIONS

OVERALL LENGTH:	194 mm
BLADE LENGTH:	82 mm
BLADE THICKNESS:	2 mm
WEIGHT:	80 g
HANDLE MATERIAL:	horn
BLADE STEEL:	12C27
LOCKING MECHANISM:	none
WHERE PRODUCED:	Italy
WEBSITE:	www.coltelleriasaladini.it

▸ **PRACTICAL AND CULTIVATED:** the curved shape of the handle lets the Fiorentino rest comfortably in your hand. The unobtrusive filework on the backspring and the silver engravings give noblesse to the knife.

Classic Nippon Folder

Similar to the significance of the Douk-Douk in France and the Mercator in Germany, is the Higonokami's status in Japan. The simple handle construction of folded sheet steel or brass is similar to that of both European folders, but the Higonokami neither has a spring nor a locking mechanism.

The Higonokami enjoys a long history reaching back to the Meiji period (1868–1912), a time of social upheavals when Japan turned from an antiquated feudal state into a modern industrial world power. This was also the period of disempowerment of the Samurai warrior caste. The demand for swords diminished; as a result many smiths turned to the production of knives. The city of Miki was a stronghold of knifesmiths, who there founded a guild in 1899. And here, too, is the origin of the Higonokami. It is said that in 1896, a hardware dealer visited the workshop of Teji Murakami in Miki in order to order a knife to be copied, which he had brought with him from Kyushu, the southwestern province of Japan. The province Higo on Kyushu inspired the naming of the knife, since "*higo no kami*" means "Governor of Higo"—an honorary title which could be inherited and disappeared with its last owner Matsudaira Katamori (1836–1893).

The knifesmith Teji Murakami is said to have added the lever-shaped blade extension (*chikiri*), which makes unfolding the knife easier. The Higonokami quickly became very popular and thus the guild in 1910, registered the name of the knife to protect themselves from imitators. Today Motosuke Nagao is seen as the only knifesmith of the guild who is allowed to legally use the brand name "Higonokami."

The Nagao-Higonokami introduced here has a carbon steel blade made of three layers (*san mai*) with a hard cutting layer of Japanese blue paper steel (*aogami*) and softer outside layers. The blade shape is an "inverted" tanto design. The blade is kept in open position by pressure of the thumb on the opening lever and by friction; in closed position it vanishes into the handle completely.

SPECIFICATIONS

OVERALL LENGTH:	173 mm
BLADE LENGTH:	75 mm
BLADE THICKNESS:	3 mm
WEIGHT:	48 g
HANDLE MATERIAL:	brass
BLADE STEEL:	3-layer carbon steel
LOCKING MECHANISM:	none
WHERE PRODUCED:	Japan
WEBSITE:	www.japaneseknifedirect.com

▸ **JAPANESE TRADITIONAL KNIFE:** the Higonokami has been produced almost without change since 1896. It served generations of Japanese school kids as a useful tool for sharpening pencils—until the government prohibited knives at schools in the 1960s. However, this did not impair the Higonokami's popularity.

For "Asphalt Cowboys"

The Stockman is an icon of American pocket knife culture. It appeared towards the end of the nineteenth century and served generations of farmers and cattle breeders as an everyday tool that could even be used for castrating bull calves in an emergency. It was a utility that wasn't treated gingerly. Almost all renowned American manufacturers and companies from Solingen produced Stockman knives in large quantities. Even today the Stockman is still one of the most popular patterns.

Over the years many variations of this multi-part knife type were created. In its classic appearance the Stockman has a lightly curved handle with bolsters at both ends. The ensemble of blades usually consists of clip point, sheepsfoot, and spey blade. The Stockman by Katz, too, is provided with this traditional blade trio. But it is miles away from a simple farmer's tool. The additional name "Executive" already evokes associations with urban suits rather than dust-covered cattle herders. The beveled, fluted, and, towards the handle end, flattened nickel silver bolsters provide the knife with an elegant appearance that qualifies the knife as a first-class gentleman's pocket knife. But since not even the Katz Stockman can deny its origins, it is like a piece of prairie that the stylish asphalt cowboy can wear in the pocket of his jacket.

Each of the three blades is provided with a false edge on its back and a generously dimensioned choil. Besides the brass liners bearing the handle scales, two additional liners take care that the spey blade has sufficient leeway towards the liner as well as the central blade. The tight back springs provide a safe feeling when working. The outstanding finish is in no way inferior to the careful construction. The transitions between handle scales, liners, and springs are finished so neatly that they can't be felt at all.

Like every Katz knife, the Stockman is made in Japan, which also explains the choice of blade steel: hidden behind the name XT80 is the proven Japanese steel AUS-8. Its high finishing standard lifts the knife well above the average.

SPECIFICATIONS

OVERALL LENGTH:	166 mm
BLADE LENGTH:	71 mm
BLADE THICKNESS:	2.5 mm
WEIGHT:	90 g
HANDLE MATERIAL:	bone
BLADE STEEL:	XT80
LOCKING MECHANISM:	none
WHERE PRODUCED:	Japan
WEBSITE:	www.katzknives.com

▸ **A PIECE OF PRAIRIE IN THE JACKET POCKET:** the first slipjoint knife of the Canadian company Katz Knives adopts the well-tried Stockman pattern. The knife, which is produced in Japan, embodies the best traditional craftsmanship.

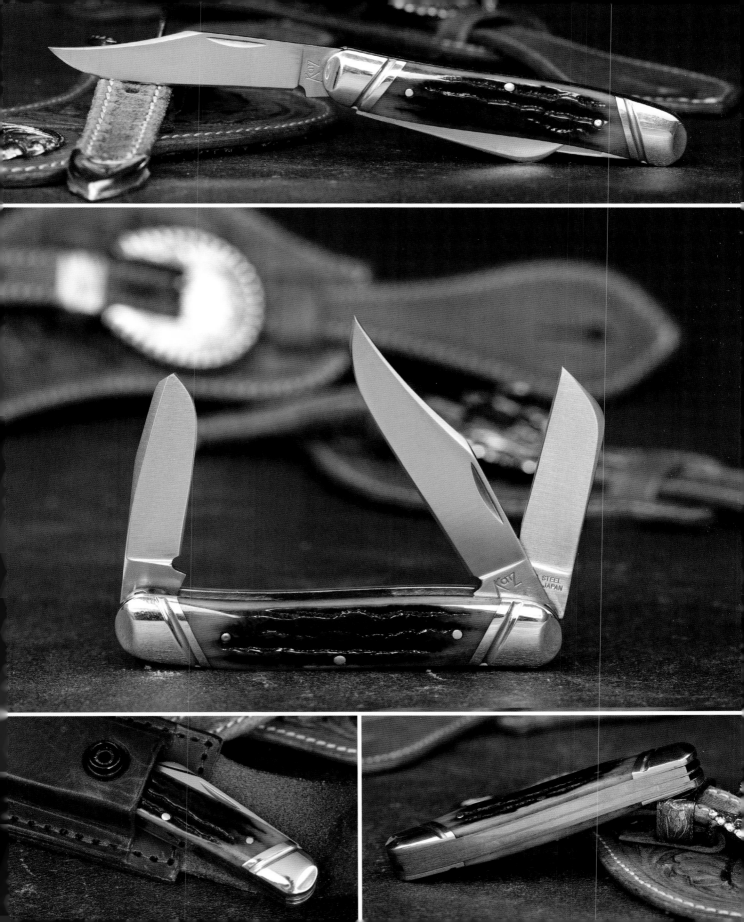

Heritage of the Algonquin

Settling the American continent is hardly thinkable without the canoe. Long before the appearance of white settlers, it served the indigenous peoples of America as a means for movement and transportation along the many streams and lakes. The Algonquin, a group of tribes in the valley of the river Ottawa, were regarded as especially skillful with respect to building canoes from the bark of birches. When fur trade between North American tribes and Europeans started in the seventeenth century, the Ottawa River became one of the most important routes on which furs and bartered goods—pocket knives were especially sought after, along with other metal wares!—were transported in canoes. The European trappers valued the fast boats as well.

The Canoe knife owes its name to the similarity of its handle shape to a canoe. In closed position, both blades are covered by the upwards pointing bolsters—an aesthetic detail deserving mention because with most pocket knives the tang protrudes a bit from the handle. The Canoe is usually provided with a duo of large and small spear point blades. Blade model 62131 by Case also follows this pattern. The model has belonged to Case's permanent delivery program since the mid-1960s. The color spectrum of bone handle scales ranges from light beige and amber-colored nuances to dark brown.

The blade etching, displaying a paddling Native American in a canoe, has been used by Case since 1974, and is still standard on the Canoe models with chromium-vanadium blades. The motif is in line with a cliché-like image tradition, not the least spread by the illustrated editions of James Fenimore Cooper's novel *The Last of the Mohicans* (1826). A highlight of the story line, playing at the time of the conflict between Great Britain and France over colonial dominance in North America, is a gripping chase with canoes. The main figures flee from a group of Huron. When they had reached a decisive lead, the white scout praised the noble son of the Mohican's chief: "You have shown, Uncas, that you know a lot about canoes of birch bark." [*Note*: This quote can't be found in the original book and is a translation taken from an unknown German source!] The company Case shows once more that they know a lot about pocket knives.

SPECIFICATIONS

OVERALL LENGTH:	157 mm
BLADE LENGTH:	65 mm
BLADE THICKNESS:	1.5 mm
WEIGHT:	77 g
HANDLE MATERIAL:	bone
BLADE STEEL:	chromium-vanadium
LOCKING MECHANISM:	none
WHERE PRODUCED:	United States
WEBSITE:	www.wrcase.com

▸ **BUOYANT:** the North American natives built their canoes of birch bark—an art in which they became real masters. The Canoe pocket knife takes its name from the handle's similarity to the shape of this type of boat.

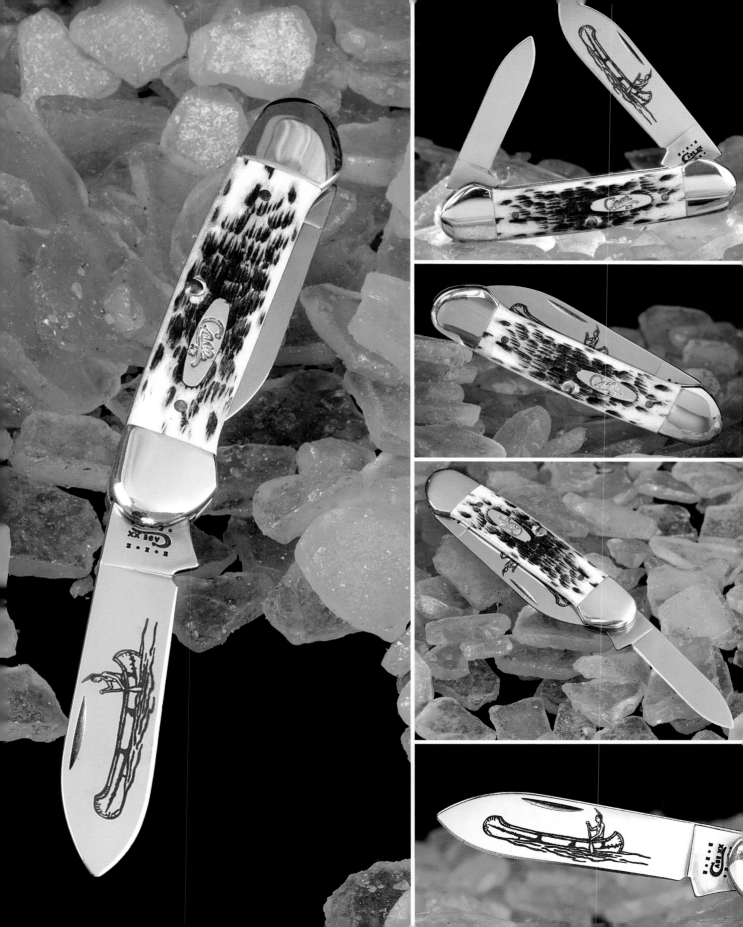

Lincoln's Pocket Knife

A whole series of anecdotes exist about US presidents and their pocket knives. The following most probably was spread by Abraham Lincoln himself: during his time as a lawyer, he was addressed by a stranger, who claimed that he possessed an item actually belonging to Lincoln. When asked how this could be the case, the stranger pulled a Barlow knife from his pocket and said he had received the knife on condition to give it to somebody even uglier than himself. To understand the punch line, you have to know that Lincoln was regarded as quite ugly by his contemporaries and that he himself often made jokes about his looks.

Like a variation on that anecdote, there is the story about Stephen Summer Phelps, a friend of Lincoln who looked like his spitting image. In the evening, Lincoln is said to have taken out a worn pocket knife Phelps disapproved of. As a reply Lincoln is said to have given the knife to his friend with the commentary that he got it under the obligation to one day give it to somebody else even more unhandsome than himself.

Whatever the truth about these amusing stories, the fact is that Lincoln, in the evening of April 14, 1865, the day of the deadly attack, had a Congress pocket knife with ivory scales and six blades with him, which most probably was made in Sheffield. Today the knife is kept in the Library of Congress in Washington.

Origin and name of the Congress pattern are historically elusive. Probably it is a design from Sheffield that was specifically meant for export to the United States where, at the beginning of the nineteenth century, the knife was especially wide-spread in the South. The slightly curved handle and square bolsters are typical for the shape of the Congress pattern. The number of blades varies; there are models known to have eight or more blades. Typical are four blades as with the Medium Congress by Case introduced here with its navy-blue bone scales and red "Case XX" label. The main blade is—not atypical for the model—a sheepsfoot blade; spear point-, coping- and pen blades complete the blade quartet.

SPECIFICATIONS

OVERALL LENGTH:	151 mm
BLADE LENGTH:	59 mm
BLADE THICKNESS:	1.5 mm
WEIGHT:	68 g
HANDLE MATERIAL:	bone
BLADE STEEL:	Tru-Sharp
LOCKING MECHANISM:	none
WHERE PRODUCED:	United States
WEBSITE:	www.wrcase.com

▸ SAD FAME: after Lincoln was murdered, in the president's pocket a Congress pocket knife with ebony scales and six blades was found, among other things. Case's Congress model makes do with four blades and bone scales.

Presidential Miniature

Dwight D. "Ike" Eisenhower, who stemmed from a German family emigrating to America as early as 1741, returned to the land of his ancestors as supreme commander of the occupation troops. The renowned and popular general was seen as the most promising candidate for the presidency in 1948, but Ike at first declined the offer because he didn't think he'd be a good politician. Four years later he competed and won the election.

Among the congratulators was J. Russell Osborne, at that time vice-president of W.R. Case & Sons, who on December 17, 1952, sent the newly elected president and his wife a letter of congratulations and a set of steak knives with mother-of-pearl handles. On January 11, 1953, nine days prior to official inauguration, the First Lady—on the letter head she appeared as "Mrs. Dwight Eisenhower"—expressed her thanks very politely for the wonderful knives. Eisenhower himself had a liking for pocket knives; his favorite model was the 63-pattern of Case. It is said that the president often presented his friends and guests of the government with this delicate, two-part gentleman's folder. He got the knives from a dealer in Texas. When Case heard of this and offered to deliver directly to Eisenhower, the president waved it aside because he wanted to continue supporting his longtime dealer.

The model was also once known under the name "Senator," but since the 1990s, it has been promoted by Case as Eisenhower. In the past, Case offered the presidential miniature, whose blades share a common back spring, in all kinds of variations. The versions with Eisenhower's signature on the blade are especially popular.

We can only speculate about what Eisenhower would have liked more: that an aircraft carrier be named after him when he was deceased, or that his favorite knife today be known under his name. Probably he would have taken a lot of time to think about it. When a young reporter once asked him how he would like to spent his retirement time, Ike answered: "Oh, young man, no rush! First of all I will put a rocking chair on the veranda. Then I will sit there peacefully for six months. After that I will slowly start rocking."

SPECIFICATIONS

OVERALL LENGTH:	126 mm
BLADE LENGTH:	47 mm
BLADE THICKNESS:	1.5 mm
WEIGHT:	34 g
HANDLE MATERIAL:	bone
BLADE STEEL:	Tru-Sharp
LOCKING MECHANISM:	none
WHERE PRODUCED:	United States
WEBSITE:	www.wrcase.com

▸ IKE'S FAVORITE KNIFE: the pattern 63 of Case is a graceful gent's folder with two pen blades. The version shown here has bone scales of the color "Golden Rod." This model has been carrying the name of the thirty-fourth US president for many years.

Powderhorn Toothpick?

Some names of traditional American pocket knives can cause headaches to knife newbies. The company Great Eastern Cutlery—abbreviated GEC—in Titusville, Pennsylvania, plays virtuously on the keyboard of historic brands, long-serving pattern names, and image-rich nicknames. An analysis brings up a lot of interesting facts.

In the present case there is first of all the brand Northfield UN-X-LD, dating back to a pioneer of the American knife industry, the Northfield Knife Company, founded in 1858, and dissolved at the beginning of the twentieth century. Northfield advertised from 1876, onward with the brand name UN-X-LD (a playful abbreviation of the word "unexcelled"). GEC revived this brand and gave it back its historical honor.

Like Case, GEC sorts its knives according to pattern numbers. The Powderhorn Jack is listed as number 12, which stands for the "Toothpick" pattern. The name "Texas Toothpick" became established at the end of the nineteenth century as a humorous nickname for a certain knife type that was especially popular in the southern United States. Today the name still represents—across company borders—a slim pocket knife with a tapered handle whose "tail" is curved inwards. In its pure form it is produced by Case as the Large Texas Toothpick. The Powderhorn Jack is a slightly more compact version that, in addition, is provided with a smaller second blade. Playing on the handle's similarity to a powderhorn, GEC gave the knife its nickname. And finally: the expression "jack knife" is a general everyday expression for practically all larger classic American pocket knives.

To call a pocket knife "toothpick" was not only meant jokingly, as British author Fanny Trollope experienced during a steamboat ride on the Mississippi in 1828. In her travel journal she writes with horror about the bad habit of her American fellow travelers of eating directly from their knives and about, "the still more frightful manner of cleaning the teeth afterwards with a pocket knife."

SPECIFICATIONS

OVERALL LENGTH:	175 mm
BLADE LENGTH:	75 mm
BLADE THICKNESS:	2 mm
WEIGHT:	91 g
HANDLE MATERIAL:	bone
BLADE STEEL:	1095
LOCKING MECHANISM:	none
WHERE PRODUCED:	United States
WEBSITE:	www.greateasterncutlery.com

▸ **COMET-LIKE RISE:** since the Great Eastern Cutlery was founded in 2006, it has developed into the favorite producer for many American collectors who value the outstanding quality of the knives. The Powderhorn Jack is no exception.

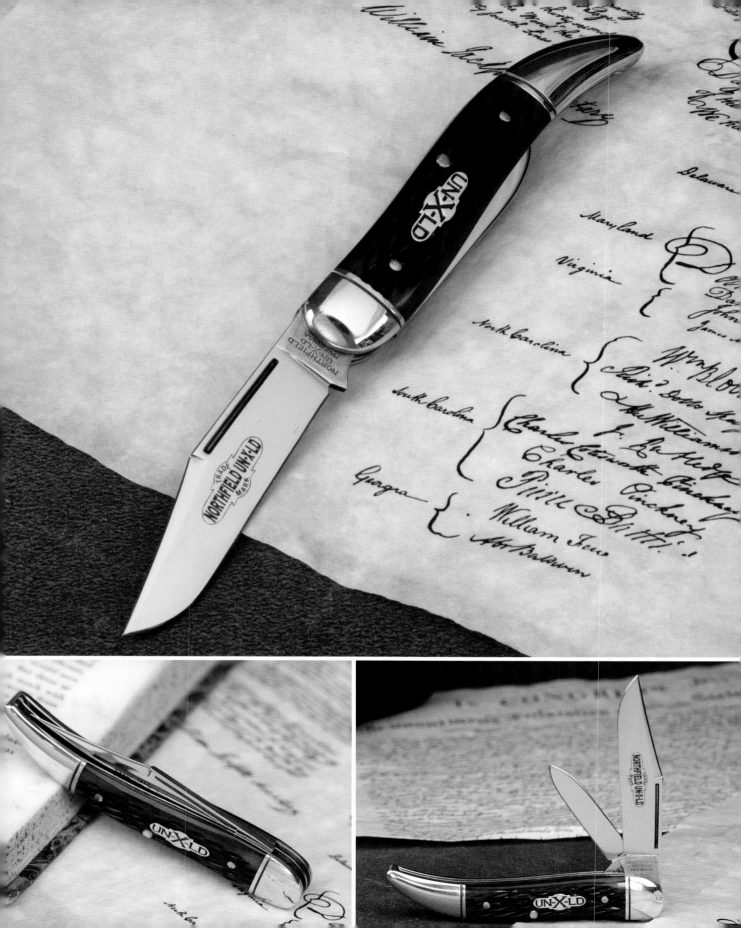

Vest Pocket Size

The very remarkable ocean inhabitant the Mola mola—commonly also called "Sunfish"—is said to be the heaviest bony fish in the world. It can reach a length of more than three meters and a weight of 2.3 metric tons. No wonder that this monstrous fish became an eponym for the largest traditional American pocket knife type. The pattern known as Sunfish is provided with a handle of up to 4½ inches length (11.4 centimeters) and two spear point blades, one of them of gigantic dimensions and the other still of more than average size.

Countless alternative names existed; the imagination of producers (and users) had no limits with respect to this pattern: Elephant Toenail, Jumbo, Old Faithful, Pumpkin Seed, Vest Pocket Axe, and more. Today the most common names are Elephant Toenail and Sunfish. Whichever name you prefer, it is in any case a giant pocket knife that was mainly used wherever heavy ropes had to be cut. Around 1900, this was the case in many industrial sectors—from wood logging to the, at that time, still young oil industry. Thus the knife was specifically marketed as "rope knife." The large blade was driven through the rope by means of a striking wood or wooden mallet, which resulted in a clean cut.

The few companies that still reissue the sunfish pattern every now and then produce foremostly for the collector's market. Great Eastern Cutlery, too, manufactures it in original size from time to time. With the model Watch Pocket Sunfish, it delivers a distinctly smaller version to the market, which actually really fits into a vest pocket. This model differs from its larger role model by not having a spear point blade as the main blade, but a somewhat stouter clip point blade.

A glance at the model number (261212) reveals that GEC lists the knife in the internal category system as "Sleeveboard" pattern. The descriptive expression is generally used for all traditional pocket knives whose handle tapers towards one side, thus emulating the shape of a sleeve ironing board. The sleeveboard variant also exists with large sunfish knives. Another model is the variant called "Swellcenter" with the handle having a little bulge in the center.

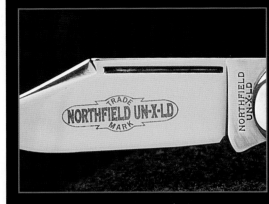

SPECIFICATIONS

OVERALL LENGTH:	129 mm
BLADE LENGTH:	51 mm
BLADE THICKNESS:	3 mm
WEIGHT:	65 g
HANDLE MATERIAL:	stag
BLADE STEEL:	1095
LOCKING MECHANISM:	none
WHERE PRODUCED:	United States
WEBSITE:	www.greateasterncutlery.com

▸ **SENSE OF HUMOR:** the typically gigantic Sunfish pocket knife has been shrunk to vest pocket size by Great Eastern Cutlery. This fancy pipsqueak is equipped with two blades and scales of stag antlers flanked by bolsters of nickel silver.

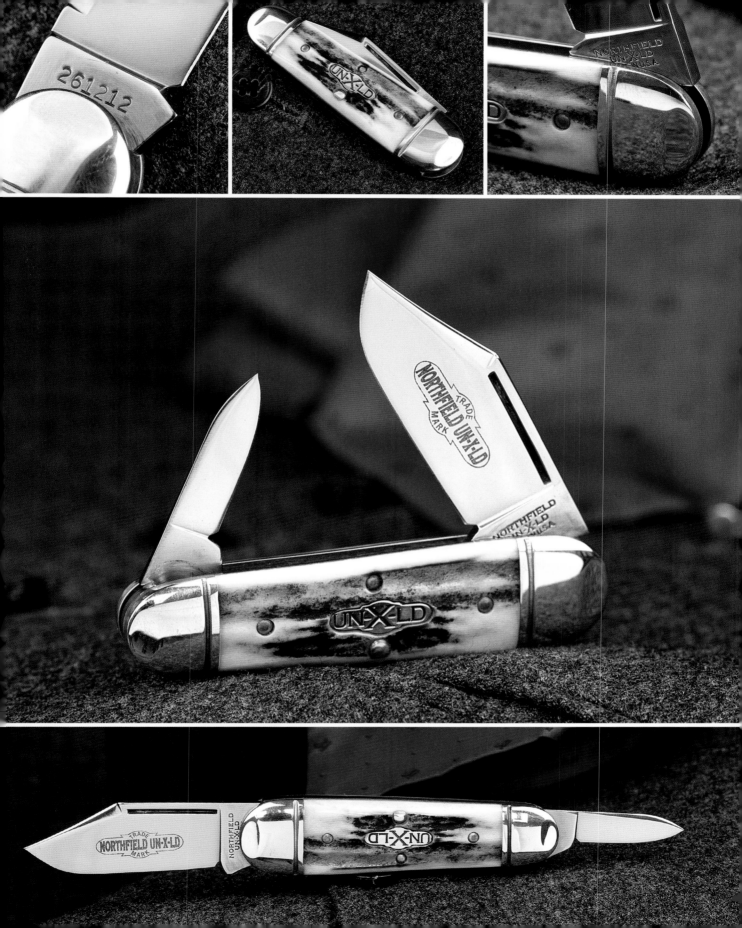

A Late Homage

The model for the first Coca-Cola bottle of 1915, is said to have been a Tiffany vase. The originally more rounded design, deriving from the more voluptuous beauty ideal of that time, was soon made slimmer for practical reasons. The famous cult bottle in turn inspired many artists and designers. It is not really surprising that one day it would also inspire a knife's handle shape.

Queen Cutlery, by the way, is neither the first nor the only producer to hit on that idea. Competitor GEC has a model with a similarly shaped handle that is marketed as Pemberton. This is a bit more imaginative and less direct, because John Pemberton was the pharmacist who invented the brown fizz.

At first glance, the Medium Coke Bottle doesn't reveal itself as a Queen knife. The blade displays the writing "Schatt & Morgan." The ricasso's frontside displays the old S & M logo, only the etching on its backside identifies the producer.

Queen has used the brand Schatt & Morgan since 1991, and this way has helped "heal" a breach in the company's history. For reasons not fully known, around 1918, the management of Schatt & Morgan Cutlery Company fired the five employees, who then in 1922, launched competitor Queen and enticed a large part of the workforce from their former employer. From that point on, Schatt & Morgan went only downhill. At the start of the 1930s, the company was ruined; factory buildings and inventory were purchased by Queen in auctions, and company founder Charles B. Morgan signed on as a traveling salesman with his former employees.

The revival of the brand Schatt & Morgan by Queen posthumously paid respect to the entrepreneurs John W. Schatt and Charles B. Morgan. In the pioneering years of the pocket knife industry, they had also laid the foundations for the later success of Queen Cutlery. Beyond historical ballast, the knife presents itself as a great gentleman's folder whose mirror-polished spear point blade with an extra long nail nick radiates class and style. The small Keystone shield decorating the stag handle scale on the frontside may as well be the keystone of this text.

SPECIFICATIONS

OVERALL LENGTH:	160 mm
BLADE LENGTH:	70 mm
BLADE THICKNESS:	2 mm
WEIGHT:	66 g
HANDLE MATERIAL:	stag
BLADE STEEL:	420 HC
LOCKING MECHANISM:	none
WHERE PRODUCED:	United States
WEBSITE:	www.queencutlery.com

▸ **LIMITED TO 400 PIECES:** this elegant pocket knife of the "Schatt & Morgan Keystone" series sets a historic link to this precursor company of Queen Cutlery. The handle's shape was inspired by a masterpiece of design history of the twentieth century.

American Queens

Many people are convinced that their local community is the most beautiful and most livable spot on Earth—and this they also want to show to the outside world. In the United States, the attribute "Queen City" was especially popular. Cincinnati, for example, in the nineteenth century was celebrated in a poem by Henry Wadsworth Longfellow as "the Queen of the West." Denver called itself "Queen City of the Plains." Fort Worth became popular as "Queen City of the Prairie." The list could be extended ad libitum. Indeed there are still three cities in the United States today named simply Queen City.

At the village boundaries of Titusville, Pennsylvania—center of Queen Cutlery since 1922—visitors are greeted with a sign that underneath the city's name has the addition "Birthplace of the Oil Industry." Here, on August 27, 1859, the first commercial oil drilling took place. But the oil boom didn't last for long. Other places turned out to be more profitable—maybe a lucky strike for Titusville. While at other places oil cities sprang up like mushrooms almost overnight and attracted corruption and crime, the village kept its civil charm.

Since Titusville, too, had the byname "Queen City," this name was quickly made part of the company founded in 1922, which still produces finest cutlery: Queen City Cutlery Company. Since January 1946, however, its name has only been Queen Cutlery Company.

As a memorial to the beginnings of company history, Queen Cutlery maintains a knife series under the label "Queen City." The items are based on their own models from the mid-twentieth century; they are—so to speak—self-referring quotes. The Swell Center Jack belongs to this series, too. It is a two-part pocket knife provided with a large and a small spear point blade, which oppose each other at the handle ends. The name of the knife is self-explaining when looking at the handle shape, which is decorated with stag scales and nickel silver bolsters.

The handy pocket knife is a cultivated everyday companion and may remind its user of the time when America still had queens.

SPECIFICATIONS

OVERALL LENGTH:	171 mm
BLADE LENGTH:	72 mm
BLADE THICKNESS:	3 mm
WEIGHT:	79 g
HANDLE MATERIAL:	stag
BLADE STEEL:	1095
LOCKING MECHANISM:	none
WHERE PRODUCED:	United States
WEBSITE:	www.queencutlery.com

▸ SELF-REFERRING QUOTE: the American manufactory Queen Cutlery can resort to a rich treasury from former periods of the company's history. The pocket knives of the Queen City series are based on their own models from the mid twentieth century.

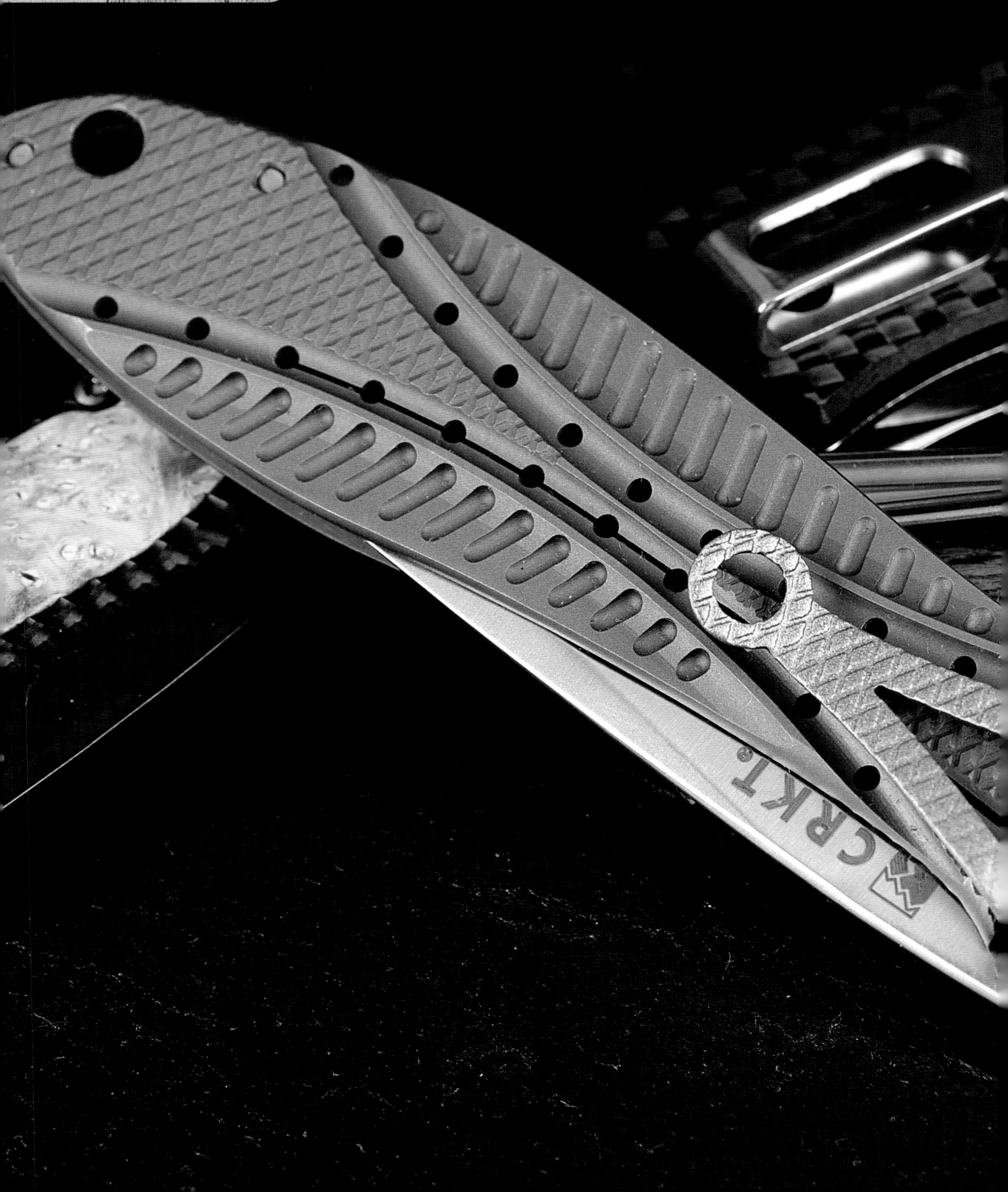
CRKT®

MODERN KNIVES

Future Classics

Less Is More

A hybrid is a mixture, a cross, or—more casually—an in-between. The Hybrid of Belgian knifemaker Filip De Coene is also a kind of in-between: this knife, available in different sizes, borrows from the traditional friction folder as well as from the kitchen knife. The result is a unique pocket knife that was awarded the Flamish design prize "Henry Van De Velde Label" in 2012.

Similar to a santoku, one's fingers rest behind the blade; the only slightly curved blade reminds you of this Japanese all-purpose knife, too. But with respect to size the Hybrid 50 could only be a miniature version of the kitchen knife. The length of the cutting edge is just 50 mm. Adding the offset between cutting edge and upper handle end to this, the result is a blade length of 60 mm. With a weight of only 48 grams, the Hybrid 50 is an absolute lightweight as well.

The knife does not need a spring or locking mechanism. The friction between tang and spacers keeps the blade open. There is no serious danger of injuries anyway, because the fingers prevent the blade from closing. When cutting, pressure on the item to be cut and the base it rests on as well as the additional pressure of the thumb on the prolonged blade tang prevent the folder from inadvertently closing.

Doing without a locking mechanism fits in with the minimalistic overall concept. The knife's silhouette convinces by its unembellished functionality. The handle back and the falling curve of the Wharncliffe blade form a lively contour against which the abrupt change in angles at the transition from blade to handle and the absolutely straight underside of the handle set a visual counterpoint. Colors and finish are finely matched: the bead-blasted titanium liners and the blasted blade harmonize very well with the sand-colored handle scales.

Filip De Coene explicitly commits himself to the aesthetic of "less is more," which he links to a strong orientation towards ergonomics and functionality. The Hybrid is the consistent implementation of this design concept and perhaps even the most uncompromising modern gentleman's folder.

SPECIFICATIONS

OVERALL LENGTH:	136 mm
BLADE LENGTH:	60 mm
BLADE THICKNESS:	3 mm
WEIGHT:	48 g
HANDLE MATERIAL:	G-10
BLADE STEEL:	ATS-34
LOCKING MECHANISM:	none
WHERE PRODUCED:	Belgium
WEBSITE:	www.ensizen.com

▸ **NO COMPROMISES:** the handy Hybrid 50 is a pocket knife that presents the oldest known folder design, the friction folder, in a modern, minimalistic design.

Something Enchanting from Solingen

Many fantastic stories have been woven around Merlin, the mysterious wizard and seer of the King Arthur saga. He is not only said to have brought the stone circle of Stonehenge from Ireland to England, he also supposedly pushed a sword into a stone block from which only Arthur could retrieve it later. This sword later breaks in battle and as a replacement the Lady of the Lake presents the legendary sword Excalibur to the king. When Merlin falls in love with this lady, she becomes his downfall: she offers him her love only under condition that he initiates her in the art of magic. As soon as she has learned Merlin's magical skills, she imprisons him—depending on the tradition—in a cave, a tree, or an invisible tower.

Whatever fascinated Solingen's knifemaker Wilfried Gorski about the stories around Merlin, the knife with the same name in any case is proof of enchanting inventiveness: The fancy gentleman's folder is provided with a patented locking mechanism (interlock). Here, an arresting bolt under tension of a spring hooks into a recess in the blade tang. At the handle back the bolt is shaped into a corrugated ramp. For closing the knife, it can be pushed comfortably with thumb or forefinger against the tension of the coil spring inside.

But the model Merlin does not only bewitch technology enthusiasts, but knife aesthetes are also rewarded: Cleanly fitted inlays of rosewood follow precisely the contours of the handle scales of stainless steel. The finish of the handle, satined crosswise, continues on the hollow grind of the blade, while the ricasso is satined lengthwise. This provides the drop point blade with a "two-tone" effect. In practical use, the knife gets points for its comfortable handling and wear-resistant blade steel.

Inspired by an article about American knifemakers, master engraver Wilfried Gorski started making his own knives in the mid-1980s. Since 1986, he is a member of the "*Deutsche Messermacher Gilde*" (German Knifemaker's Guild). As his main job he runs a company for plastics technology in Solingen and only makes very few knives per year. All the more pleasant that Böker produces the Merlin in series, which provides a lot of enthusiasts with the possibility of buying a knife in Gorski design.

SPECIFICATIONS

OVERALL LENGTH:	175 mm
BLADE LENGTH:	72 mm
BLADE THICKNESS:	2.6 mm
WEIGHT:	82 g
HANDLE MATERIAL:	rosewood
BLADE STEEL:	N690
LOCKING MECHANISM:	interlock
WHERE PRODUCED:	Germany
WEBSITE:	www.boker.de

▸ **SYNTHESIS OF TECHNOLOGY AND AESTHETICS:** not only the stylish design of the model Merlin, but the patented interlock as well, are the brainchildren of the renowned knifemaker Wilfried Gorski of Solingen.

Universal Folding Puukko

Whoever goes hunting or fishing in the far north of Europe usually takes a fixed blade. The famous *puukko*, the belt knife of the Finns, is seen as the embodiment of the Nordic knife whose suitability for use has been proven for centuries. Because of this, some Nordic manufacturers have ignored the market for folders for a long time and discovered it only with a delay. Interesting here are the different approaches. The Swedish company Karesuando, for example, makes pocket knives on their own and uses materials typical for the region, such as curly birch and reindeer antlers. The folders of the Norwegian company Helle, too, stay close to tradition. Finnish neighbor Martiini in turn acts more shirt-sleeved by importing folding knives from China, which don't have any reference to the region.

The company Brisa, founded in Jakobstad, Finland, in 1996, is no classic knife producer but mainly a dealer in knifemaking supplies. In addition, it distributes a small assortment of fixed blades and folders under the brand name EnZo. But the successful model Trapper as well as the folding knives Birk 75 and PK70 are not made in Finland but in Taiwan.

The EnZo Birk 75 is far more than just a modern folding interpretation of a *puukko*—quite often it is advertised as such. Though the Scandinavian grind may be seen as reminiscent of Nordic tradition, the Birk 75 is an all-round pocket knife, comparable in design and layout to similar models of Spyderco, also produced in Taiwan. Examples are the Sage series, the Gayle Bradley, or the Nilakka which, too, is marketed as "folding *puukko*."

The special grind in combination with S30V steel provides an outstanding cutting ability. The handle scales are made of resistant G-10 carbon fiber laminate. The gently curved handle belly provides comfortable handling. Due to its open construction, cleaning the knife is easy. The blade can be opened effortlessly with a single hand by means of the thumb studs on both sides of the blade. And it is arrested reliably with the well-adjusted liner lock. With a bit of training, the knife can be opened and closed again by a left-handed person, too. The only disadvantage: the deep-carry pocket clip can't be relocated.

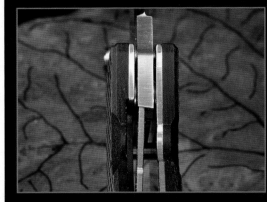

SPECIFICATIONS

OVERALL LENGTH:	179 mm
BLADE LENGTH:	75 mm
BLADE THICKNESS:	3 mm
WEIGHT:	105 g
HANDLE MATERIAL:	G-10/carbon fiber
BLADE STEEL:	S30V
LOCKING MECHANISM:	liner lock
WHERE PRODUCED:	Taiwan
WEBSITE:	www.brisa.fi

▶ **NORDIC STYLE OF THE FAR EAST:** the EnZo Birk 75, produced in Taiwan, is marketed by the Finnish company Brisa as a foldable Puukko for outdoor use. But in fact it also proves itself as a practical pocket knife for urban everyday use.

Innovation Instead of Imitation

The title "*Meilleur Ouvrier de France*" (best craftsman of France)—often abbreviated MOF—is a highly respected national award. Extraordinary achievements in different areas of craftsmanship have been rewarded with this honorary title since 1924. The competition stands under the patronage of the French Ministry of Labor. The criteria of the professional juries in the individual categories are demanding and the competition pressure is enormous. In the end only the best of the best are honored. Handing over of the medals to the MOC prize winners takes place at the Sorbonne; afterwards there is a celebratory ceremony in the Élysée-palace in the presence of the French president.

Anyone who once wins the prize awarded for lifetime can count himself/herself lucky. Knifemaker Jean-Pierre Sucheras, born in 1956, received the renowned award for the first time in 2004, in the pocket knife category. Three years later he received it once more in the hunting knife category.

The model Actilam T3, introduced in 2014, arose from the collaboration of Jean-Pierre Sucheras and Pascal Jodas, whose company Arno produces forged parts and industrial blades. Both friends are connected by a passion for aesthetically and technically innovative products. The Actilam T3 is also committed to this approach. It wins over by its clear contours and innovative locking mechanism. The back spring is twisted over a length of about two-and-a-half centimeters, then widens towards the blade in an oval. This spring head is shaped in such a way that it latches in a recess of the tang when the knife is opened. But the trick is that the spring is not lifted for unlocking, but has to be pushed sideways with the thumb.

To underline the fact that the blade is forged (and not blanked), the elongated depression on one side of the blade towards the back is left unfinished. The stainless blade steel X50CrMoV15N is hardened to 58-60 HRC and can easily be re-sharpened. The blade has a width of two millimeters, a flat grind, and excellent cutting properties. The stable bearing of the blade prevents any play. The scales of carbon fiber fit well to the knife's innovative concept.

SPECIFICATIONS

OVERALL LENGTH:	197 mm
BLADE LENGTH:	85 mm
BLADE THICKNESS:	2 mm
WEIGHT:	64 g
HANDLE MATERIAL:	stainless steel/carbon fiber
BLADE STEEL:	X50CrMoV15N
LOCKING MECHANISM:	see text
WHERE PRODUCED:	France
WEBSITE:	www.sucheras-coutelier.fr

▸ **SOPHISTICATED INGENUITY:** it is always surprising to see the new locking mechanisms thought up by knife designers. To unlock the blade of the Actilam T3, the spring doesn't have to be lifted but pushed sideways.

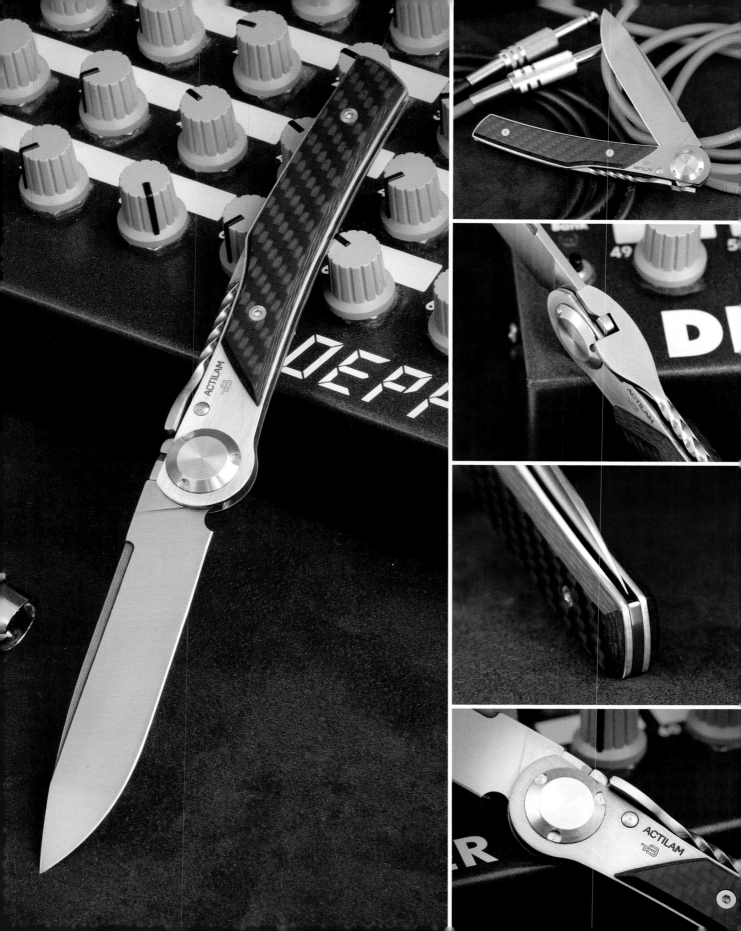

The Blissful Life

Sometimes knives are meant to illustrate philosophical thoughts: Occam's Razor, for example, is a metaphor for the principle to make do with the smallest number of hypotheses for the explanation of a phenomenon. And German philosopher Johann Gottlieb Fichte once described the "pure I" as "a thing falling back onto and into itself similar to a folding knife." From Martin Heidegger the famous quote has been passed down that you can't lose God in the same way you lose a pocket knife. His disciple Hans-Georg Gadamer deepened this thought into a kind of negative proof of being: "After losing a utility you have long been used to, such as a pocket knife, it proves its existence by making you feel its absence constantly." Yes, even great minds sometimes tend towards mundane topics.

If philosophy can't make do without knives, it is only just if in turn a knife company takes its images from the history of philosophy. The Coutellerie Robert David, founded in Thiers in 1919, produces the usual repertoire of French knife art from A as in Alpin to Y as in Yssingeaux. But one model is out of the ordinary: the Épicurien is a slim pocket knife whose shape imitates a fountain pen. By means of the clip at its side it can be worn comfortably in the inside pocket of your jacket. Because of its unobtrusive appearance, the knife indeed fits well into business and office life. There are more than thirty handle materials you can choose from. In addition, the customer can personalize the knife even further by means of an engraving on blade or spring.

An Epicurean is a man of pleasure. But it would be wrong to interpret the teachings of Epicurus as a pleading for an excessive and sensuous lifestyle. This strict thinker was already confronted with this mean-spirited misunderstanding during his lifetime. The blissful life, according to Epicurus, consists of achieving peace of mind, a state free from desire, fear, and pain.

By the way, there was a Frenchman hidden inside the Greek Epicurus, "*avant la lettre*" (before the expression existed), as a letter to a friend reveals: "Please, send me a bit of cheese so I will be able to have a delicious meal, when I am in the mood for it." This sounds like culinary frugality, not like unrestrained gluttony.

SPECIFICATIONS

OVERALL LENGTH:	210 mm
BLADE LENGTH:	90 mm
BLADE THICKNESS:	2 mm
WEIGHT:	66 g
HANDLE MATERIAL:	olive wood
BLADE STEEL:	12C27
LOCKING MECHANISM:	liner lock
WHERE PRODUCED:	France
WEBSITE:	www.robert-david.com

▸ **THE BIRTH OF A POCKET KNIFE FROM THE SPIRIT OF A FOUNTAIN PEN:** the Épicurien can only be recognized as a knife at a closer look. Its unspectacular and socially acceptable looks make it an ideal folder for everyday business.

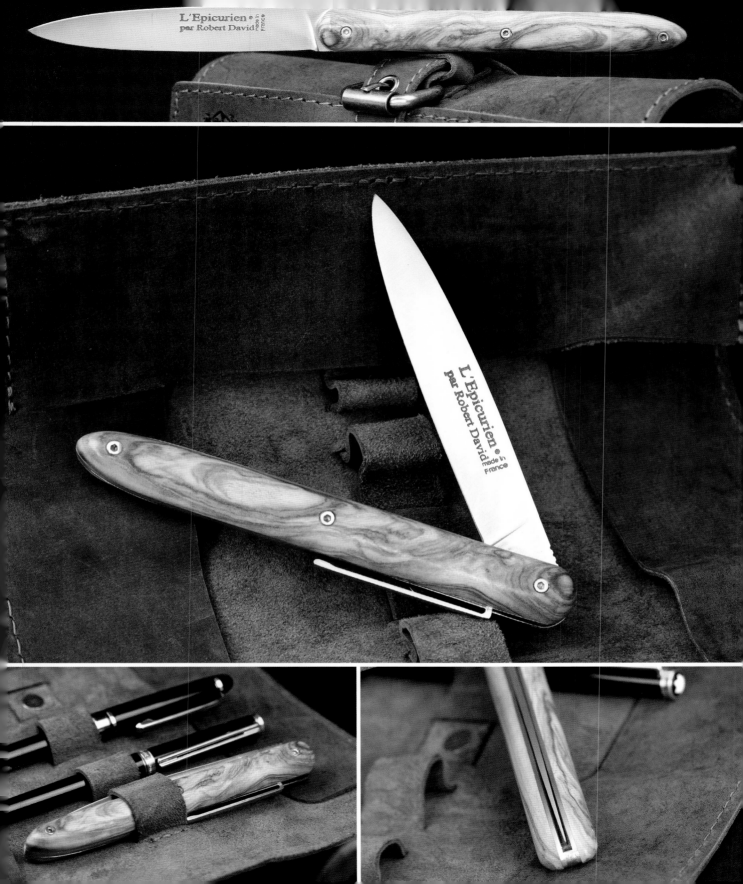

From Galluchat to Galuchat

Madame de Pompadour would have enjoyed this variant of the Le Thiers knife by Claude Dozorme. The powerful mistress of King Louis XV was said to be very keen on valuables decorated with ray skin.

Around 1748, the Parisian leather artisan Jean-Clauden Galluchat invented a method for tanning and refining ray skin, which allowed it to be processed like normal leather. From then on, the exotic material was used for the production of sheaths, casings, and pouches and also for the embellishment of small makeup boxes, jewel cases, chests, and small pieces of furniture. It is said that Madame de Pompadour was Galluchat's best customer.

Among the many hundreds of interpretations the Thiers knife has found during the last two decades, the model of Claude Dozorme stands out especially by its choice of handle material. The ray leather is located between the liners and an outer cage of stainless steel. With a handle width of approximately 18 mm and a handle length of 124 mm, the knife is also well-suited for people with large hands.

While the blade of classical Thiers knives is not locked, this model has a liner lock. By means of the small nose at the tang, which protrudes a bit at the handle's end in closed position of the blade, the knife can even be opened singlehandedly with a bit of skill. The axis screw can be adjusted using an included special tool.

The manufactory Claude Dozorme, founded in 1902, received awards for its innovations several times. In addition to the Galuchat, the company offers many more variants of the popular Le Thiers: from a minimalistic liner lock version and a slipjoint with ball bearings to a model with a sophisticated opening mechanism.

In Japan, the handles of samurai swords were already covered with ray skin centuries before the time of Pompadour. In France, the name of the leather artisan Galluchat found its way into the language (unfortunately one letter was lost to a writing error): "*galuchat*" is the French word for ray and shark skin.

SPECIFICATIONS

OVERALL LENGTH:	218 mm
BLADE LENGTH:	94 mm
BLADE THICKNESS:	3 mm
WEIGHT:	134 g
HANDLE MATERIAL:	ray skin
BLADE STEEL:	X50CrMoV15
LOCKING MECHANISM:	liner lock
WHERE PRODUCED:	France
WEBSITE:	www.dozorme-claude.fr

▸ **UNUSUAL AND HIGH-END:** the incredible diversity of the Thiers knife, established in 1994, is demonstrated by this model with ray skin from Claude Dozorme. The material's authenticity is guaranteed by a certificate.

Le THIERS ®
Par Claude DOZORME ®

Fabriqué en France

CLAUDE DOZORME
FABRIQUÉ EN FRANCE
DEPUIS 1902
THIERS
www.dozorme-claude.fr

Véritable
Galuchat

Knife of the Year

Among the wares and treasures that Portuguese sailors had brought back to their homeland since the discovery of the sea route to India, the Indian rhino unloaded at Lisbon on May 20, 1515, was probably the most exotic import. The animal was a gift of the governor of Portuguese-India to King Manuel I of Portugal. In expectance of a bloody spectacle, on June 3, 1515, the king let the rhino compete against a young elephant in an arena. But there was no fight between the two heavyweights, because the elephant took to its heels at an early stage in the encounter.

At the same time, the recently crowned French monarch Francis I was plagued by other worries: the Swiss disputed French dominance in Northern Italy. The conflict peaked in the Battle of Marignano in mid-September, 1515, in which Francis I successfully drove off the Swiss. On the way back to Paris, the king is said to have rested in Thiers, which by then was already a famous knife city. Whether fact or anecdote, the French king in any case impressed Manu Laplace, born in Clermont-Ferrand in 1971, so much that later he named his first knife atelier in Thiers "La Coutellerie François 1er."

Manu Laplace first worked as a car mechanic and on a minesweeper before he found his real calling, the art of forging knives. As a great-grandchild of Gaston Cognet, the inventor of the legendary Douk-Douk knife, this path was almost set by destiny. Today Manu Laplace together with a small team produces this beautifully shaped pocket knife that is named after the year of the Battle of Marignano—a knife of the year in the very sense of the word!

In the year 1515, the masur birch of Karelian origin would have been almost as exotic in France as the Indian rhino in Portugal. The characteristic dark crescent-shaped inclusions in the bright wood turn the knife handle into an interesting eye-catcher. The handle end is finalized by two bolsters of stainless steel separated from the wood by black fiber inlays. The unobtrusive filework on the handle's back even continues on the inside. The highly polished blade is arrested by means of a liner lock.

SPECIFICATIONS

OVERALL LENGTH:	200 mm
BLADE LENGTH:	80 mm
BLADE THICKNESS:	2.8 mm
WEIGHT:	120 g
HANDLE MATERIAL:	masur birch
BLADE STEEL:	12C27
LOCKING MECHANISM:	liner lock
WHERE PRODUCED:	France
WEBSITE:	www.1515-laplace.com

▶ **TIMELESS DESIGN WITH TIME STAMP:** the events of 1515 impressed Manu Laplace so much that he named his knife after the year.

Dominated by the Sign of the Trident

The sea and beautiful knives are the passions of Thierry Henriot, the enthusiastic yachtsman and creative head behind the brand name Neptunia. While other French knife producers stick to the long-established traditions and produce Laguiole and other regional knives in countless variations, the knives of Neptunia are all dedicated to maritime topics. A few years ago, the brand was still an insider's tip in the noble yacht clubs from Monaco to Saint-Tropez. But in the meantime it has found enthusiasts all over the world.

Classic ship hulks, historic dinghies such as the famous "Yole de Bantry 1796," or legendary racing yachts serve as a source of inspiration for the knife designs. In cooperation with designer Thierry Kayo, beautifully-shaped luxury knives are created that are produced by selected French manufactories in manual work. The model Dorry is based on a traditional dory (also written "*dori*" or "*doree*"), a lightweight fishing boat used in fishing close to the coastline, along the Atlantic coast from New England to Newfoundland, as well as an auxiliary boat on larger fishing vessels. This boat type from the eighteenth century is characterized by its construction with flat bottom, pointed bow, and small stern. The knife's handle design incorporates these characteristics: the beautifully-grained kingwood scales have a center bulge and taper towards the handle end. The inclined handle butt with lanyard hole practically forms the stern area.

The shape of the blade is unusual as well. It is a sheepsfoot blade reduced to its geometrical basic shape. With this blade shape the Dorry joins the tradition of sailing knives without being typecast to this role. The blade, ground flat from the back downwards, is also fit for use on land. The straight blade shows its capabilities especially when peeling and cutting without extra support. The 12C27 steel offers a good compromise between edge retention and easy re-sharpening.

Lovers of maritime lifestyle will spontaneously like the Dorry. Landlubbers may perhaps need a second glance to discover the beauty of this knife.

SPECIFICATIONS

OVERALL LENGTH:	165 mm
BLADE LENGTH:	65 mm
BLADE THICKNESS:	2 mm
WEIGHT:	72 g
HANDLE MATERIAL:	kingwood
BLADE STEEL:	12C27
LOCKING MECHANISM:	none
WHERE PRODUCED:	France
WEBSITE:	www.neptunia.fr

▸ **MARITIME FLAIR:** the knives of Neptunia are dedicated to the sea and seafaring. Name and shape of the Dorry go back to a traditional fishing boat with flat bottom which has been used for centuries in deep-sea and coastal fishery.

Farewell to the Province

In Marcel Proust's famed novel *In Search of Lost Time* (initially translated as *Remembrance of Things Past*) Madame Verdurin, smug host of a Parisian saloon, reacts shocked to the announcement of a friend to spend a few days in the Auvergne: "In the Auvergne? Do you want to be eaten up by fleas and bugs?" In the noble Paris of the "Fin de Siècle" this region was seen as provincial and underdeveloped. Because of the pressing poverty, many people had left the Auvergne in the nineteenth century. On the search for jobs, many tried their luck in the cities; some people from the Auvergne established themselves successfully as gastronomes in the capital of France.

The demure charms of the volcanic landscape today attract a lot of touring cyclists and hikers, among them many completing a leg of the Road to Santiago on the Via Podiensis. On the Route des Fromages d'Auvergne many tasty kinds of cheese can be discovered. The good cuisine is widely known far beyond state borders anyway—as are the famous Laguiole- and Thiers knives.

The company Perceval succeeded, beyond all regional knife folklore, in conquering a market segment that is especially prestigious: Perceval provides first-class restaurants worldwide with high-quality kitchen knives and table cutlery. Whether in London, Singapore, Tokyo, Copenhagen, Melbourne, Hong Kong, or Dubai—head chefs and gourmets cut with knives from Thiers. Since the former award-winning chef Yves Charles has been directing the fate of the knife manufactory, it has left behind all provinciality and has won an international reputation, proved by coveted prizes and awards.

With the L-series, Perceval has created a beautifully-shaped pocket knife that connects tradition and modernity. While the models L-09 and L-10 with their prolonged tang still relate to the Piémontais style, the model L-08 abstains from historic reminiscence and presents itself as a modern folder with liner lock mechanism. The open-frame construction of the handle makes cleaning easier and keeps the weight down. Due to the cutting properties of the flat-ground blade in modified sheepsfoot design, the L-08 is well-suited as a table knife to take with you to all the restaurants that are not yet equipped with knives of Perceval.

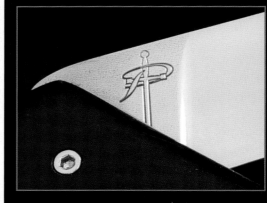

SPECIFICATIONS

OVERALL LENGTH:	205 mm
BLADE LENGTH:	95 mm
BLADE THICKNESS:	2.5 mm
WEIGHT:	75 g
HANDLE MATERIAL:	ebony
BLADE STEEL:	19C27
LOCKING MECHANISM:	liner lock
WHERE PRODUCED:	France
WEBSITE:	www.couteau.com

▸ **FOR THE OPTIMAL TREAT:** some French people use their own knives in a restaurant. It is questionable whether this trend will become established. However, with a Perceval L-08 you don't have to be embarrassed in any gourmet temple in the world.

One Nation, One Knife

When Yves Charles, as a Parisian chef awarded with one Michelin star, went to Thiers in 2005, he just wanted to equip his restaurant with cutlery. In the end he bought a complete knife factory.

But first things first: at the end of 2004, Yves Charles was sitting in his restaurant together with friends for whom he had prepared duck breast. Some friends used the restaurant's cutlery to cut the meat, others pulled their own knives from their pockets, which turned out to be examples of the model Le Français of Atelier Perceval. When the top chef realized that these pocket knives were cutting much better than the restaurant knives, his interest was caught. In the following year he drove to Thiers in order to develop a knife in cooperation with Perceval that should have the same excellent cutting properties as the Le Français. After several meetings with Eric Perceval, who had founded the manufactory in 1996, not only was the now legendary table knife "9.47" launched, but Yves Charles was also the new owner of the Atelier Perceval. Three years later, he gave up his restaurant in order to tend to the knife business exclusively.

The design of the Le Français is inspired by a French model of the seventeenth century. But the knife's simple elegance fits into all time periods and follows no fashion. Focusing solely on the essential, a harmonically designed pocket knife was created, whose name sounds as immodest as self-confident: The Frenchman! It remains to be seen whether this knife one day will achieve the same status as an Opinel or Laguiole knife. The liner lock folder has an open handle construction. Various materials are available for the three-dimensionally constructed handle scales. The knife owes its good cutting properties, which impressed Yves Charles so much, to its two-and-a-half-millimeter thin drop point blade with flat grind, for which the stainless Swedish steel 19C27 was used.

This knife, without doubt, fulfills what Antoine de Saint-Exupéry wrote about perfection: "Perfection is achieved not when there is nothing more to add, but when there is nothing left to take away."

SPECIFICATIONS

OVERALL LENGTH:	199 mm
BLADE LENGTH:	90 mm
BLADE THICKNESS:	2.5 mm
WEIGHT:	62 g
HANDLE MATERIAL:	juniper
BLADE STEEL:	19C27
LOCKING MECHANISM:	liner lock
WHERE PRODUCED:	France
WEBSITE:	www.couteau.com

▸ **A KNIFE FOR THE GRANDE NATION:** while the classic French regional knives bear the names of their places of origin, the Le Français by Atelier Perceval strives to represent the entire country. The maximum claim is implemented with minimum means.

In Memoriam Bob Loveless

On September 2, 2010, legendary American knifemaker Bob Loveless died. One month later, Benchmade announced the takeover of the company Lone Wolf Knives. Both events are not directly linked, but nevertheless there is a certain connection: the City Knife of Lone Wolf, an elegant gentleman's folder, was designed by Bob Loveless. With Bob Loveless' death and the acquisition of Lone Wolf, the City Knife vanished, but had a kind of reincarnation in the Dweller by Fantoni. The Italian knife producer of Maniago had already produced the City Knife for Lone Wolf; the Dweller is a reworked version, for which Massimo Fantoni, son of company founder Renzo Fantoni, is responsible.

The three most important modifications: in contrast to the City Knife, the Dweller has no bolsters. A finger guard was added which hides the blade tang in closed position. And the liners of stainless steel were exchanged for brass liners.

The new model name leaves leeway for interpretation; it only makes sense in combination with the old one. As "city dweller," the pocket knife would be clearly positioned as a folder for townsfolk. Since it is a slipjoint knife, legal carry should be possible in most towns of the world. Like its predecessor, the Dweller is provided with a half-stop, which improves the safety during handling. The blade shape matches the original design of Bob Loveless, who preferred this drop point shape.

Before Renzo Fantoni took to the knife industry in 1980, he had worked as an engineer in the turbine industry. Thus he knows a lot about the complex requirements with respect to steel. For the Dweller, he chose the stainless Sandvik steel 19C27, distinguished by its wear resistance. For the handle scales, several attractive wood types are on offer. The finish of the knife is solid, as usual.

Fantoni was the first Italian company to have knives designed by renowned knifemakers. The Dweller is a worthy homage to the City Knife and its creator, the great Robert Waldorf Loveless.

SPECIFICATIONS

OVERALL LENGTH:	160 mm
BLADE LENGTH:	66 mm
BLADE THICKNESS:	2.3 mm
WEIGHT:	56 g
HANDLE MATERIAL:	snakewood
BLADE STEEL:	19C27
LOCKING MECHANISM:	none
WHERE PRODUCED:	Italy
WEBSITE:	www.fantoniknife.com

▸ **URBAN DESIGN:** the Dweller, made in Italy, is based on the City knife of American knifemaking legend Bob Loveless. The cultivated getleman's pocket knife is respectable in every cosmopolitan surroundings.

Bravo! Da Capo!

That a pocket knife can serve well in an opera house is attested by an anecdote about Giuseppe Verdi: when the composer conducted a rehearsal of *Aida* at the Vienna Court Opera, the coordination between on-stage music and orchestra caused problems. The conductor on the stage could not see Verdi's movements with the baton. Quickly the maestro climbed onto the stage, pulled out his pocket knife, and enlarged the opening in the decoration designed for this purpose.

Surprising ingenuity was also repeatedly shown by the Italian company LionSteel. The family-led company invested in state-of-the-art CNC machines and cooperates with top designers in order to create pocket knives that delight technically as well as aesthetically. The prize-winning model SR-1 convinced the professional world as well as the users by its new handle construction: instead of the usual construction with handle scales, the handle including the frame lock is milled from a single titanium block. The advantage: fewer individual parts and tighter tolerances! The system, called RotoBlock, which prevents the locking spring from being overstretched and from inadvertent unlocking, is a functional innovation, too.

Other brands as well now profit from the production know-how of the Italians: DPx Gear in the United States, Bastinelli in France, and Pohl Force in Germany have single product lines or even their entire program produced by LionSteel.

The Opera doesn't fit into the category of hi-tech titanium folders but represents the classical style also belonging to LionSteel. The pocket knife was designed by Italian knifemaker Massimo Salice Sanna who designed other products for LionSteel, too. Whoever thinks of magnificient stage magic and the airs and graces of a diva when hearing the name is wrong. The Opera is a sound and solid back lock folder of elegant simplicity. Provided with a hollow-ground and satined D2-blade, the knife masters small and medium-sized cutting tasks with flying colors. The Opera is available in several versions. The model with wooden handle scales is a pure gentleman's pocket knife; the version with G-10 scales, made with a glance at the US market, has additional thumb studs and a pocket clip.

SPECIFICATIONS

OVERALL LENGTH:	177 mm
BLADE LENGTH:	74 mm
BLADE THICKNESS:	3 mm
WEIGHT:	67 g
HANDLE MATERIAL:	olive wood
BLADE STEEL:	D2
LOCKING MECHANISM:	back lock
WHERE PRODUCED:	Italy
WEBSITE:	www.lionsteel.it

▸ **NOT ONLY FOR OPERA FANS:** the knife's name leads you to expect dramatic passion and boasting gestures. But far from that! The Opera is pure understatement. It presents itself in the finest gentleman's manner as a self-effacing pocket knife of style.

Sociable Design

When talking about Italian design, one spontaneously thinks of racy sports cars and glamorous fashion, maybe even of the likeable Vespa motor scooter by Piaggio. Italian design can be simple and functional, like the famous Olivetti typewriter MP1, or excite emotions, as with the Lamborghini Gallardo. It is never trivial. This is also valid for the cutting tools of Italian knife designers.

Sergio Consoli found his fulfillment only late in life. Although fascinated by knives since childhood, he only started to make knives at the age of forty. Now the self-trained Consoli belongs to the best artisan knifemakers of Italy. For Maserin, the family business founded in Maniago in 1960, he designed an elegant folder that is available in several versions. The most attractive eye-catcher without doubt is the model 402/RV with handle scales of dyed burl wood.

The silhouette of the opened knife forms a harmonic line without embellishments. A playful counterpoint is created by the decorated margins of the liners, which surround the entire handle like a seam of waves. The serrations on the back spring take up this wave movement which continues as thumb ramp on the blade back.

The drop point blade is provided with a flat grind and is locked by means of a back lock. The choice of blade steel makes the expert smile: S35VN for a gentleman's folder of this size is comparable to what is called "overpowered" with a car. Such a high-quality steel is not really necessary, but it is good to know that in case of an emergency—to stay with the image—you still have some more horsepower under the hood.

The Italian designer and interior decorator Aldo Cibic coined the expression "sociable design" ("*design conviviale*"). Although this expression belongs to the area of home decor, it can be transferred to the Maserin Consoli: if this pocket knife is put on the table during a social get-together with good food and wine, then it will inevitably become a topic of the conversation. It will make the rounds and inspire all kinds of considerations—about design, beauty, and sometimes even about life. Not many knives exist that succeed in this.

SPECIFICATIONS

OVERALL LENGTH:	175 mm
BLADE LENGTH:	73 mm
BLADE THICKNESS:	3 mm
WEIGHT:	84 g
HANDLE MATERIAL:	burl wood
BLADE STEEL:	S35VN
LOCKING MECHANISM:	back lock
WHERE PRODUCED:	Italy
WEBSITE:	www.maserin.com

▶ **PLAYFUL ELEGANCE:** the outline of this gentleman's knife is without embellishments; the wave-like decorations on the liners and back spring, in contrast, radiate extravagance.

Nomen Est Omen (the Name Speaks For Itself)

The following malicious *aperçu* (*bon mot*) is known of the English author Charles Dickens: that he doesn't know the "American gentleman" and has to ask God for forgiveness for even putting together both words. The expression "gentleman," which was shaped in England, described a man who was socially elevated by his aristocratic ancestry, who didn't have to work, and thus could focus on refining his mind and manners. Today this expression is largely independent of the social status and in fact points to a style of life that cannot be captured in strict rules, to respectful composure, cultivated manners, and unobtrusive elegance.

Thus, if a knife manufacturer markets a knife with the name "Gent," it puts the knife into a cultural context which it hopefully lives up to. Is the Viper Gent of the company Tecnocut, founded in Maniago in 1987, an appropriate knife for the gentleman? This question can be answered in the affirmative without hesitation.

The design was made by the Italian Fabrizio Silvestrelli who has been working as a full-time knifemaker since 2004, and has designed a whole slew of gentleman's knives for Tecnocut. According to his own statements, he loves to combine traditional and modern style elements, which is proven by the Gent: the handle design is similar to that of the Napoletano, an old regional knife. But the locking mechanism is the modern button lock system, which is based on the well-established liner lock principle. The difference is that the liners are inlaid in the handle scales and thus the locking liner is not directly accessible. The push button visible from the outside is the end of a bolt that presses the locking liner aside in order to unlock the blade. The mechanism works reliably and provides a lock free from any play.

Ziricote is a kind of tree that grows in Central America. The hard tropical wood is distinguished by its dark brown color interspersed with black wavy lines. As an alternative, Tecnocut offers brighter wood types. The flat-ground blade of stainless N690Co steel impresses by its remarkable cutting powers. The blade back is rounded and finished as a false edge over half of its length.

SPECIFICATIONS

OVERALL LENGTH:	172 mm
BLADE LENGTH:	75 mm
BLADE THICKNESS:	2.5 mm
WEIGHT:	90 g
HANDLE MATERIAL:	ziricote
BLADE STEEL:	N690Co
LOCKING MECHANISM:	button lock
WHERE PRODUCED:	Italy
WEBSITE:	www.viper.it

▸ **MADE IN MANIAGO:** during the last century, the northern Italian blade city gave birth to some very innovative knife producers such as Fox, LionSteel, Maserin, and Tecnocut. The Viper Gent—as the name already suggests—is a gentleman's knife by Tecnocut.

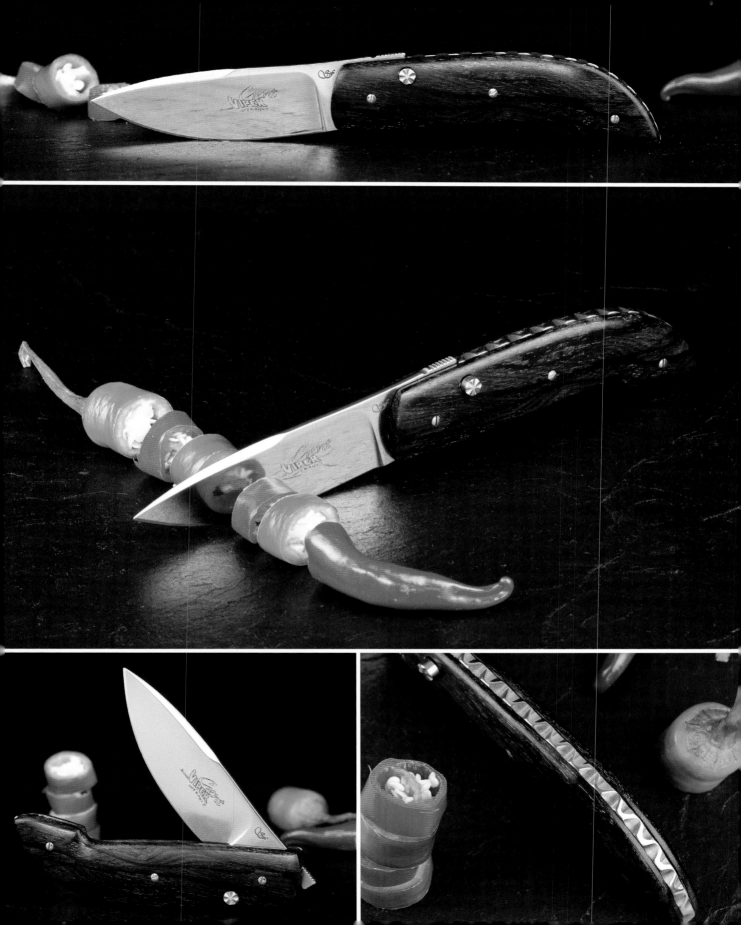

Be Like Bamboo

In Japan, because of its fresh green color, bamboo is seen as a symbol of purity. In former times it was an important material for the production of items for daily use and of samurai weapons such as spears, lances, and bows. In the early nineteenth century the giant grass was imported to Europe from China and Japan. In Germany, bamboo was mainly becoming part of horticulture and autograph books: "Be like bamboo, bend and sway graciously as the wind desires and you will never break."

The handle shape of Mcusta's pocket knife with the unpoetic model name MC-0074D is also based on a piece of bamboo. But the handle scales are made of cocobolo wood. Mcusta is one of several brands of the company Marusho Kogyo, founded in Seki in 1964. Besides high-quality pocket knives, the company produces scissors and kitchen knives, too.

The city of Seki looks back on a long tradition of the art of forging: the first smiths settled there in the thirteenth century already. During the Muromachi period (about 1336 to 1573), supposedly there were more than 300 swordsmiths in Seki. But when Japan's warrior caste of samurai was abolished at the end of the nineteenth century, the old craftsmanship lost its importance as well. As a consequence, the production shifted from edged weapons to cutting tools for which Seki is still famous today.

The brand name Mcusta is an artificial word created from "machine custom knives," which underlines the ambitious claim of the company to produce serial knives of the same high quality as delivered by custom knives. Mcusta uses highly precise laser-cutting systems and CNC milling machines, but assembly and finishing are done manually. The consistently flawless workmanship justifies Mcusta's international reputation as a premium brand.

The suminagashi blade of the knife is typical for Mcusta: thirty-three-layer damascus is added on both sides to a cutting core of VG-10 steel. The blade can be opened singlehandedly by means of the blue anodized thumb stud and is solidly arrested by a firmly securing liner lock. The blade's movements can be adjusted effortlessly by means of a simple slotted screw. The knife is delivered together with a belt pouch of Nishijin cloth, which is similar to brocade.

SPECIFICATIONS

OVERALL LENGTH:	164 mm
BLADE LENGTH:	70 mm
BLADE THICKNESS:	3 mm
WEIGHT:	56 g
HANDLE MATERIAL:	cocobolo
BLADE STEEL:	suminagashi
LOCKING MECHANISM:	liner lock
WHERE PRODUCED:	Japan
WEBSITE:	www.mcusta.jp

▸ **DOUBLE TRADITION:** the city of Seki stands for the century-old forging tradition; the Nishijin silk weaving stands for the long-established textile art of Japan. The depicted pocket knife of the brand Mcusta is produced in Seki and is provided with a belt pouch of Nishijin cloth.

The Titan as Gentleman

The choice of a product name has to be considered well because otherwise an embarrassing faux pas may happen—as was the case with the model MR2 of Toyota, whose name amused the French very much because "MR deux" sounds dangerously close to "*merde*" ("shit").

The name "Kronos" is also not very well chosen for a gentleman's knife: in the world of Greek gods, Kronos was the titan who—incited by his mother Gaia—emasculated his father Uranos with a sickle. You may not want to be reminded of this all the time when working with this knife. But with the exception of this forgivable slip regarding the choice of name, the Moki Kronos is harmonious to the smallest detail.

The Japanese knife manufactory Moki, based in Seki, is a family business with a history of more than a hundred years and stands as a synonym for meticulously produced pocket knives. Its origins reach back to the year 1907, when the later company founder Moichi Sakurai as a thirteen-year-old boy was sent to a knifesmith for training. A son of Moichi, who had the nickname Moki, later founded his own company, which in 1980, was renamed Moki Knife Co. and is now led by Satoru Sakurai, a grandchild of Moichi. By far, the largest part of the production is made up of third parties' orders for international companies.

The model Kronos, marketed under their own name, is a back lock folder with handle scales of burnt bone. Striking features are the elongated bolsters of stainless steel, which form a gentle finger groove. Despite the traditional construction and materials, the knife has an unobtrusive modern appearance mainly due to the slim design of lines. All in all, the Kronos presents itself as the distinguished cutting tool for the cultivated man.

To save the honor of the Greek titan Kronos, it has to be said that, after disempowering his father, he became the founder of the Golden Age in which humans were friends of the gods and led a life free from sorrows. It is said that one day he was put into chains by his son Zeus and abducted to a paradise-like place—the Fortunate Isles or Isles of the Blessed—where he is said to still live today.

SPECIFICATIONS

OVERALL LENGTH:	164 mm
BLADE LENGTH:	70 mm
BLADE THICKNESS:	2.5 mm
WEIGHT:	62 g
HANDLE MATERIAL:	bone
BLADE STEEL:	VG-10
LOCKING MECHANISM:	back lock
WHERE PRODUCED:	Japan
WEBSITE:	www.moki.co.jp

▸ **EXCURSION IN GREEK MYTHOLOGY:** the model Kronos of the Japanese manufactory Moki is named after the youngest of the Titans—perhaps a somewhat questionable designation. But the pocket knife itself is beyond all doubt.

Play of Light

Mother-of-pearl—also called nacre—is a fascinating natural material. It is created as an inner layer within the shells of different species of bivalves and snails and serves as a protection against predators. Seen under the scanning electron microscope, the material appears as a layered structure composed of the mineral aragonite. Each lets the light pass through partially and partially reflects it. By the superposition of incoming and reflected light (interference) the characteristic iridescent play of light is created, which has enchanted humans from different cultures since times unknown. Very early in history, mother-of-pearl was already used for the production of jewelry and for decorating objects of daily use. In the Polynesian world of islands, the polished shells were even used as a currency for a long time.

Over the centuries, mother-of-pearl, along with silver and ivory, was used as material for the scales of especially classy pocket knives. But since high-quality mother-of-pearl is expensive and has to be processed extremely carefully, it was replaced with plastics in later years. For serial knives, mother-of-pearl seems to be totally out of fashion today; only among custom knives is it still a permanent feature.

An exception is made by the Japanese company Moki, which provides a lot of its classy gentleman's pocket knives with mother-of-pearl. The model Serapis—named after an Egyptian-Hellenistic deity—presents the colorful, iridescent, and precious material in a non-standard way: rectangular platelets of white and dark mother-of-pearl are put together like intarsia inlaid into the handle. The darker pieces, which originate from the black-lip pearl oyster, shine in all colors of the rainbow.

Even though the Serapis looks like a precious piece of jewelry, it is foremost a thoroughly functional cutting tool. The flat-ground and finely stropped blade of Japanese VG-10 steel leaves no doubt about that. Safety and ergonomics are also not neglected: the blade is arrested without any play via back lock; handling of the knife is very comfortable despite its small size. And—as can be expected from Moki—the production quality is at the highest level.

SPECIFICATIONS

OVERALL LENGTH:	148 mm
BLADE LENGTH:	63 mm
BLADE THICKNESS:	2.3 mm
WEIGHT:	42 g
HANDLE MATERIAL:	stainless steel/mother-of-pearl
BLADE STEEL:	VG-10i
LOCKING MECHANISM:	back lock
WHERE PRODUCED:	Japan
WEBSITE:	www.moki.co.jp

▸ **DAZZLING PLAY OF COLOR:** photos can hardly depict the iridescent effect of mother-of-pearl. Depending on the visual perspective, the material shines in hundreds of different hues. The inlays on both sides of the Moki Serapis are put together intarsia-like from bright and dark mother-of-pearl platelets.

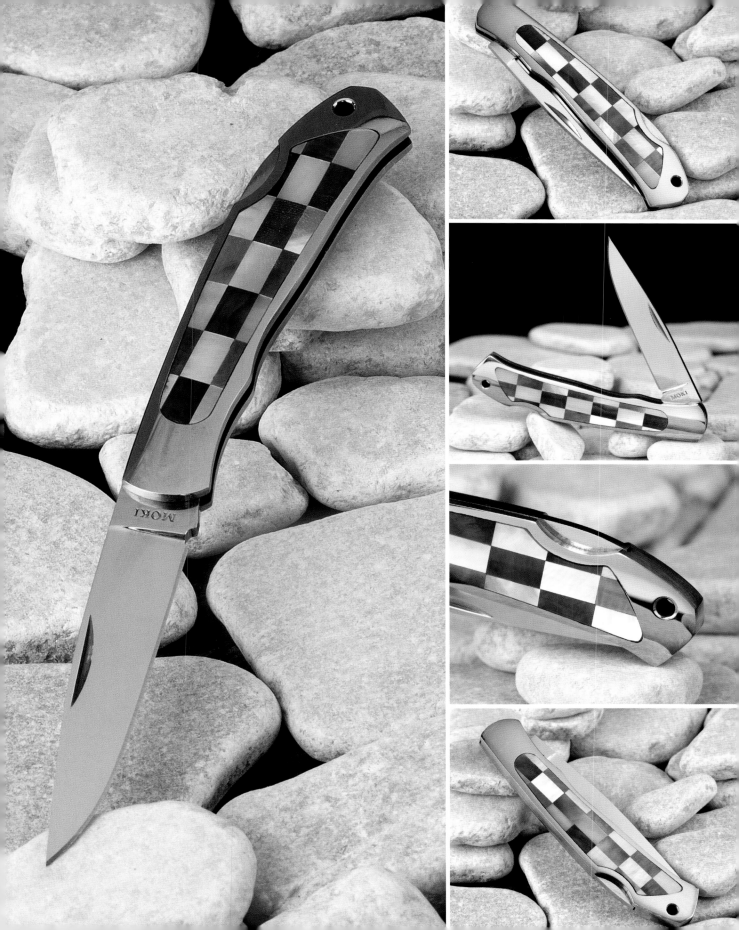

Japan and the West

After centuries of seclusion, in 1853, Japan was forced by warships to start trading with the West. In the following years an almost euphoric interest in art and craftsmanship of Japan arose in Europe. Artists such as Claude Monet, Vincent van Gogh, Paul Gauguin, Henri de Toulouse-Lautrec, and Gustav Klimt were inspired by Japanese multi-colored woodblock prints and drawings. The art critic Philip Burty, in 1872, coined the expression "Japonism" for the prevailing Japan fashion.

A Rockstead knife represents a lot of the things in Japanese culture that have fascinated Western admirers. Aesthetic subtlety, respectful bow to tradition, and the absolute will for perfection are mirrored in the knives that are only marketed in small numbers and have set new benchmarks with respect to serial production. Rockstead thus also speaks of "serial custom knives."

The SHU-CB is a handy folder with a closed handle construction of titanium. A hard carbon coating protects the titanium surface from scratches. This knife is the only Rockstead model provided with a button lock. The convex grind on both sides of the blade (*honzukuri*) is based on traditional Japanese sword models. The stainless high-performance steel ZDP-189 is brought up to an impressive hardness of 67 HRC by means of precise heat treatment. The combination of steel and blade geometry provides extraordinary sharpness as well as edge retention. Aficionados, in addition, value the expertly done mirror polish, which is unrivaled in the entire knife industry.

A very special show of blossoms is displayed by the engravings on the handle scales. Depicted here are blossoms of the Japanese apricot (*Prunus mume*) which already blooms in January and once was more popular than the famous cherry blossoms celebrated in spring each year (*hanami*, "flower viewing").

By the way, it was the German physician, ethnologist, and botanist Philipp Franz von Siebold who, between 1823 and 1829, researched Japan's world of plants systematically for the first time. In the times of Western gunboat politics, he vehemently fought for the peaceful opening of Japanese borders.

SPECIFICATIONS

OVERALL LENGTH:	194 mm
BLADE LENGTH:	84 mm
BLADE THICKNESS:	3.2 mm
WEIGHT:	100 g
HANDLE MATERIAL:	titanium
BLADE STEEL:	ZDP-189
LOCKING MECHANISM:	button lock
WHERE PRODUCED:	Japan
WEBSITE:	www.rockstead.jp

▸ **HI-TECH AESTHETICS:** the SHU-CB convinces by means of its harmonious contour lines and minimal production tolerances. Each detail fits perfectly—from the decorative blossom engraving, the milled-out portions on the handle back, to the blade's perfect centering.

Blade City Phnom Penh

The history of the Cambodian company Citadel started in the neighboring country Vietnam. When Dominique Eluere opened the first French restaurant in Saigon, he discovered that no steak knives could be obtained in the entire country. The attempt to import them failed because of Vietnamese customs. What to do? The inventive Frenchman entrusted regional craftsmen, a smith and a carpenter, with making the knives. His guests liked the handmade steak knives so much that they wanted to buy them. In no time Dominique Eluere was not only a gastronome but also a knife dealer.

It didn't stop with steak knives. Kitchen knives were added, and soon Dominique Eluere designed all kinds of knives. In 1999, he founded the company Citadel in Pnomh Penh, the capital of Cambodia. The company is no longer an insider's tip. Around fifty employees produce a wide range of knives and edged weapons of different style in manual work—even very elaborate katana, which are the pride and joy of Citadel. The quality of the products is on par with international standards.

The model Monterey is an excellently made folder with liner lock. There is nothing specifically Cambodian about it; the design is European as is the blade steel, and maple burl wood is a popular handle material used throughout the entire world. The unobtrusive decorations give the knife a French appearance. The thin handle scales have three-dimensional contours and are set apart from the liners of stainless steel by a bright fiber layer. The mirror-polished blade is ground convexly and provided with a finely worked false edge that runs along almost the entire blade back.

By the way, the knife is named after the small coastal town of Monterey, California, which once thrived off fishing sardines, and was the backdrop for the famous novels *Cannery Row* and *Tortilla Flat* by John Steinbeck. The poor fellows and likable scalawags in the novels most probably would have traded a knife such as the Monterey immediately for a few gallons of wine. But in real life its owner probably will hardly part with such a beautiful piece.

SPECIFICATIONS

OVERALL LENGTH:	185 mm
BLADE LENGTH:	80 mm
BLADE THICKNESS:	3 mm
WEIGHT:	126 g
HANDLE MATERIAL:	maple burl wood
BLADE STEEL:	N690Co
LOCKING MECHANISM:	liner lock
WHERE PRODUCED:	Cambodia
WEBSITE:	www.knives-citadel.com

▸ **UNIQUE SUCCESS STORY:** the company Citadel, founded by Frenchman Dominique Eluere in 1999, is based in Cambodia. The first employees were village smiths and carpenters. Today they are masters of the fine art of cutlery craftsmanship.

A Gentleman Wears Red

Keith Derkatz grew up on a wheat farm in Canada. His father took him on hunts while he was still a kid. He still has a passion for the wilderness and for hunting. Over the years another passion was added: because he was not satisfied with the hunting knives available on the market, Keith Derkatz designed his own models. Provided with a keen sense of business, he founded the company Katz Knives in 1991; the serial production of his knives was farmed out to Japanese companies. Since then he has designed about 150 knives in many variations. The bandwidth ranges from fixed outdoor and hunting knives to tactical folders and even pretty gentleman's knives.

The original designs and the high production quality gave Katz Knives a faithful basis of international customers. On the German market, the products have had a rather fluctuating success—not the least because of frequently changing sales partners. A special handle material has asserted itself as an unofficial, but nevertheless distinctive brand sign: cherry wood. With a few exceptions, almost all knives are available with scales of this stylish wood, ranging in color from deep wine to bright signal-red.

The model Bob Kat, too—the name being a wordplay on "Katz" and "bobcat," a North American species of lynx—has a scale of cherry wood on the frontside that is attached to a brass liner. Other materials are available as an alternative. The backside of the compact knife is made up of a liner of satined stainless steel with a broad clip curving across it, meant to serve as a money clip. Some users even see the money clip as the primary function with the blade being only a useful add-on. As an option, Katz offers a belt buckle which also serves as a fastener for the knife—a way of carrying it surely not according to everybody's taste.

To provide more room for the hand, part of the blade gives way to a finger groove so the Bob Kat can be held with four fingers. The fine serrations on the blade's back provide a safe rest for thumb or forefinger. The blade is made of the stainless Japanese steel AUS-6—Katz uses the name XT70 for it. It has a hollow grind and is arrested by means of a back lock.

SPECIFICATIONS

OVERALL LENGTH:	122 mm
BLADE LENGTH:	57 mm
BLADE THICKNESS:	2 mm
WEIGHT:	75 g
HANDLE MATERIAL:	cherry wood
BLADE STEEL:	XT70
LOCKING MECHANISM:	back lock
WHERE PRODUCED:	Japan
WEBSITE:	www.katzknives.com

▸ **TWO-FOLD UNITED STATES:** for some the Bob Kat is a pocket knife with money clip, for others a money clip with blade. Regardless of one or the other, the compact pipsqueak is a purposeful accessory in your trouser pocket.

Sweden's Solingen

During the heyday of the blade cities Solingen and Sheffield, the steel processed there was won from iron ore originating mainly in Sweden. But the Swedish iron ore mines provided for the forges in their own country, too. The city Eskilstuna developed into a center of the forging craft. The first forge powered by water is documented for the year 1485. In the seventeenth century, King Charles X Gustav forced the development of metal processing in Eskilstuna by ordering Reinhold Rademacher, born in Riga, to build several forges, some of which are still operating as museums. During the Industrial Revolution, the Swedish cutlery industry boomed; many companies settled in the "*stålstaden*" (steel city)—that's how Eskilstuna was called at that time. But around the mid-twentieth century the downfall of knife production started there.

Of the more than forty companies in Sweden's Solingen only the company founded by Hadar Hallström in 1882 survived. Since 1917, it bears the name EKA—short for *Ekilstuna Kniffabriks Aktiebolag*. Over many decades its production focused on a wide pallet of multi-part pocket knife models. When Torbjörn Evrell took over management of EKA in 1946, the range of products was streamlined radically. In 1970, the Swede series was started, which is still successful today. It consists of a number of simple but robust folders. Later on, fixed blades for outdoors use were added and in the meantime the program was even broadened to include tactical folders. A specialty of EKA is flat gentleman's knives in slipjoint construction, which can have other companies' logos to be used as means for advertisement.

The model Classic 5 is very close to the classical gent's knife. It has a very flat construction, too, but is provided with a back lock. The handle scales of stainless steel are decorated with ornaments similar to Celtic knot patterns. In the center of the handle scales, on one side is the royal coat of arms, on the other EKA's logo. The all-purpose drop point blade of 12C27 steel is ground flat starting at the back.

SPECIFICATIONS

OVERALL LENGTH:	150 mm
BLADE LENGTH:	59 mm
BLADE THICKNESS:	2 mm
WEIGHT:	79 g
HANDLE MATERIAL:	stainless steel
BLADE STEEL:	12C27
LOCKING MECHANISM:	back lock
WHERE PRODUCED:	Sweden
WEBSITE:	www.eka-knivar.se

▸ **SWEDISH GENTLEMAN'S KNIFE:** the brand EKA today stands mostly for robust outdoors knives. But initially the company, founded in 1882, was a classic manufactory of pocket knives. The Classic 5 follows this tradition—a timeless gent's knife of high-end appearance and feel.

Retro Style and Inner Values

Retro is in—and has been for so many years already that some retro trends are already out again. It was just a question of time until the retro wave would also reach the knife world. The Fällkniven GP is virtually the "New Beetle" among the pocket knives: according to its looks it could have originated at a time when greetings from the "summer resort" were still transmitted via postcard and hippies were avant-garde. But on its inside, the folder is equipped with modern technology.

The model GP—the "Gentleman's Pocket Knife" as it's explicitly called by Fällkniven—has traditional handle scales of wood and stainless steel bolsters; the blade is opened via nail nick in the old-fashioned way. But in contrast to a pocket knife of the old school it is not a slipjoint folder but has a liner lock. The construction is screwed together so that the blade movement can be adjusted, if necessary. Only the lanyard lug at the handle end is riveted with a metal pin and renders the screws of the handle scales useless, because the scales can't be taken apart without destroying the pin. But since all parts were put together without any gap, you will hardly have to unscrew the handle scales completely.

The blade steel is not retro at all. Fällkniven is known for having highest demands with respect to the ability to re-sharpen and to hold an edge. Here, the Swedish company has faith in the products of Japanese steel producer Takefu. The Lam.CoS steel—an abbreviation for "Laminated Cobalt Special steel"—is a three-layer laminate steel: the blade's inner cutting layer is made of CoS steel with a hardness of 60 HRC. The outer layers consist of the more flexible 420J2 steel.

But not only the steel originates in Japan. Fällkniven has its entire range of models produced in the land of the rising sun. But the Swedes love to play hide and seek: the land of origin is neither mentioned on knives, on packaging, or in the catalogs. The reasoning goes: in a globalized industry this information is not really important. But maybe it just fits better with the renowned position of being purveyor of the royal court if the company presents itself as a purely Swedish one.

SPECIFICATIONS

OVERALL LENGTH:	180 mm
BLADE LENGTH:	78 mm
BLADE THICKNESS:	3 mm
WEIGHT:	97 g
HANDLE MATERIAL:	cocobolo
BLADE STEEL:	Lam.CoS
LOCKING MECHANISM:	liner lock
WHERE PRODUCED:	Sweden
WEBSITE:	www.fallkniven.com

▸ **ELEGANT RETRO-DESIGN:** the GP—short for "Gentleman's Pocket Knife"—at first glance looks like a traditional pocket knife. But the hi-tech blade steel and liner lock prove that it is a modern gent's folder.

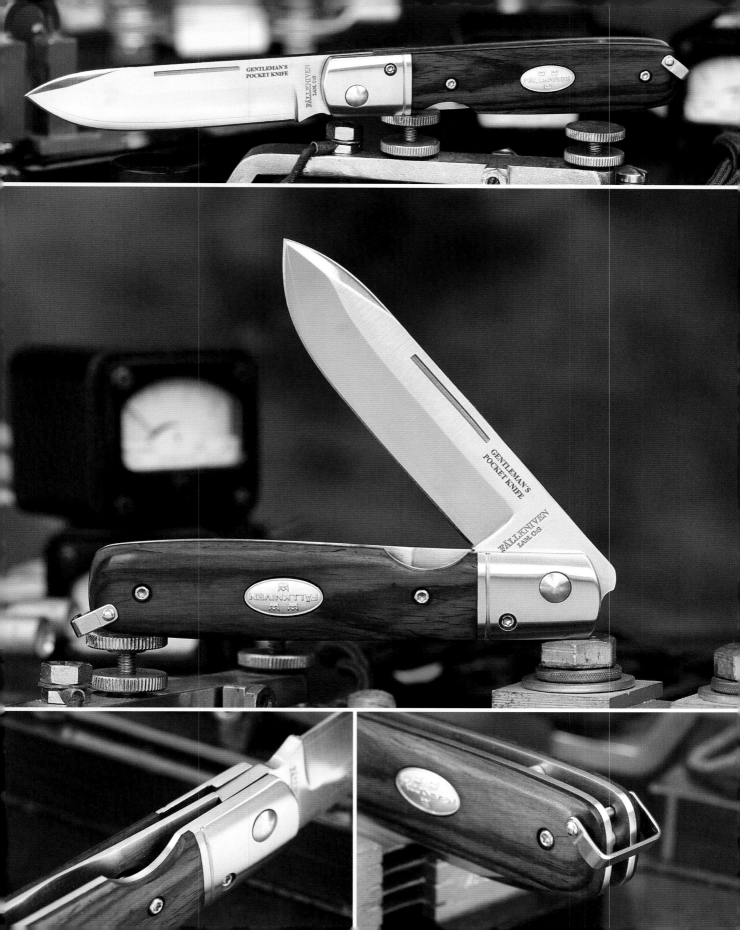

Nordic Charms

The village of Karesuando is located about 300 kilometers north of the polar circle. It is a remote place in the historic province of Lapland, surrounded by the vastness of the Arctic tundra. Here is not only the northernmost church of Sweden, but also the small factory of Karesuando Kniven. The company's philosophy is deeply rooted in the traditional Sami culture, Lapland's native population. They lived as nomads until the 1940s, following the reindeer with their families. The animal's fur and leather were used for the production of clothing, shoes, and tents; from bone and antlers, small tools and jewelry were made. In the everyday life of the Sami, knives were essential for survival.

The fixed blade hunting and fishing knives offered by Karesuando in a multitude of variants continue the regional tradition. Only masur birch and reindeer antlers are used for knife handles—natural materials that are able to withstand even extreme coldness. Company head Per-Erik Niva is especially proud that all production steps are made in the company's own factory: from blanking the blades to sewing the leather sheaths.

The model Singi—named after a mountain peak—is the first folding knife in the company's history. The handle scales of masur birch as well as other details point to the knife's regional origin. The lanyard (the cord at the handle's end) consists of two intertwined strings of reindeer leather knotted together behind a piece of reindeer antler. The round handle inlay with the Karesuando logo is made of reindeer antler as well.

The slightly curved handle whose back tapers towards the blade rests comfortably in the heel of your hand. The finger groove, shaped by two massive bolsters of stainless steel, allows for slip-free work. The stainless damascus was made by the Swedish company Damasteel. The blade is provided with a Scandinavian grind and is arrested by means of a back lock. A practical leather belt pouch completes the equipment.

The Singi is a pocket knife from the realm of the midnight sun and polar lights. Thus it will probably appeal especially to those people who have a weakness for Nordic culture and landscape.

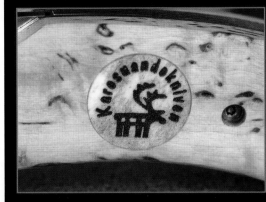

SPECIFICATIONS

OVERALL LENGTH:	195 mm
BLADE LENGTH:	80 mm
BLADE THICKNESS:	2 mm
WEIGHT:	126 g
HANDLE MATERIAL:	masur birch
BLADE STEEL:	damascus
LOCKING MECHANISM:	back lock
WHERE PRODUCED:	Sweden
WEBSITE:	www.karesuandokniven.com

▶ **A PIECE OF LAPLAND:** the producer Karesuando is known for fixed blades in Nordic style. For the folder Singi, enhanced with a damascus blade, the Swedes also used natural materials, such as masur birch and reindeer antlers.

Swiss Precision Work

The AGR Carbon has constructed a bridge between Switzerland and the United States. The abbreviation AGR stands for the initials of none other than legendary American knife designer and dealer A.G. Russell, who made his first knife at the age of nine. The rest is history: in 1974, he became the first member of the *Knife Digest* Cutlery Hall of Fame; in 1988, he became member of the *Blade Magazine* Cutlery Hall of Fame. As owner of a mail order business he has been an established constant since 1964. In between, A.G. Russell even engaged himself in Germany when in 1975, he took over the failing company Carl Bertram in Solingen (at that time owner of the brand "Hen & Rooster"), which vanished from the market completely just a few years later.

The AGR is produced by the Klötzli Messerschmiede, a Swiss family business since 1846, today led by Hans Peter Klötzli in the fifth generation. He himself learned his trade at Victorinox. Today the manufactory plays in the same league as Chris Reeve or William Henry.

The folder's delicate handle construction consists of two scales and an arresting spring; all components are made of titanium. On the front side, the 3D weave pattern of the carbon fiber inlay is an optical highlight. The handle's matte titanium finish harmonizes well with the satined blade, which is provided with a super sharp hollow grind done by hand. The choice of blade steel evokes associations with another American legend: Bob Loveless preferred the Japanese ATS-34 for his custom knives and other knifemakers followed his lead.

Swiss precision work can also be seen in the carefully adjusted liner lock and the incomparably smooth blade movement. By means of the thumb stud, the knife can be opened single-handedly. The open handle construction and choice of material turn the AGR into a lightweight of just 50 grams. For carrying, the pocket clip or the provided nappa leather pouch are well suited.

The AGR is not the only cooperation between Klötzli and an American knifemaker. Designs of Michael Walker and Ernest Emerson, too, were implemented in Switzerland in an ingenious way.

SPECIFICATIONS

OVERALL LENGTH:	152 mm
BLADE LENGTH:	65 mm
BLADE THICKNESS:	3 mm
WEIGHT:	50 g
HANDLE MATERIAL:	titanium/carbon fiber
BLADE STEEL:	ATS-34
LOCKING MECHANISM:	liner lock
WHERE PRODUCED:	Switzerland
WEBSITE:	www.klotzli.com

▸ **NOT EVERY SWISS KNIFE WAS MADE BY VICTORINOX:** this gent's folder, designed by A.G. Russell, is Swiss precision engineering at its best made by knife forge Klötzli of high international renown.

A Contradiction in Itself?

A Swiss pocket knife with only a single blade could almost be called a *"contradictio in adiecto,"* since the reputation of the world-famous knife is based on the multitude of different tools assembled in confined space. But they existed and still exist: Swiss pocket knives provided with one blade only. The model 0.8000.26 of the Pioneer series belongs to them.

A lot of books have already been written about the Swiss pocket or officer's knife—internationally abbreviated SAK ("Swiss Army Knife"). Since 2014, this knife type is only produced by the company Victorinox, founded by Karl Elsener in 1884. The competitor Wenger, taken over by Victorinox in 2005, was allowed to have a model policy of their own until the end of 2013. But since the users can hardly find any difference between both brands, Victorinox decided to give up the brand Wenger altogether and to integrate the most popular models into their own program. In the meantime Victorinox has developed into a trendy international lifestyle brand, not only marketing knives but also watches, clothing, travel baggage, and perfume.

The Pioneer series was introduced in 1957, and was the first knife series of Victorinox equipped with handle scales of aluminum; it was served as a basis for the model Soldier 1961. The handle scales of aluminum—called "Alox" by Victorinox—are not only more robust and also more slip-proof than the usual plastic scales, due to their checkered surface, but they also appear more precious and modern. Sometimes Alox scales in the colors red, blue, green, orange, or black are used for limited special editions with a special appeal to the large crowd of Victorinox collectors.

Victorinox knives are often categorized according to their handle length. The single-blade Pioneer falls into the class of 93 mm and thus offers enough room for a mid-sized hand. The minimal equipment of the knife should not tempt its owner to use the blade as a universal tool. It still holds: a blade is made for cutting—not to be a lever, screwdriver, or drill. Whoever needs a tool with many functions will find an almost limitless choice at Victorinox.

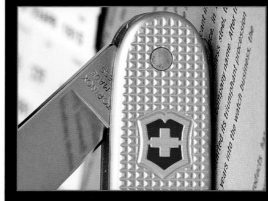

SPECIFICATIONS

OVERALL LENGTH:	163 mm
BLADE LENGTH:	70 mm
BLADE THICKNESS:	2.5 mm
WEIGHT:	44 g
HANDLE MATERIAL:	aluminum
BLADE STEEL:	1.4110
LOCKING MECHANISM:	none
WHERE PRODUCED:	Switzerland
WEBSITE:	www.victorinox.com

▸ **UNUSUAL MINIMALISM:** the one-part pocket knife of the Pioneer series by Victorinox seems to strictly contradict the principle of a Swiss Army Knife. But because of its low weight and flat construction it is ideal as a gentleman's folder.

Typically Untypical

When the American company Benchmade joined the knife market at the end of the 1970s, it was still named Bali-Song and its reputation was based solely on the folding knives with the same name, which over here are better known as butterfly knives. After the reestablishment as Pacific Cutlery Corporation in 1988, two years later the change of name into Benchmade Knife Company and the move from California to Oregon followed.

Butterfly knives are still one of the pillars of the production program, but meanwhile Benchmade covers a much broader spectrum, ranging from tactical folders and everyday folding knives to outdoor knives with fixed blade. In addition, Benchmade produces knives for other brands such as Harley-Davidson and Heckler & Koch. The most interesting models are created in cooperation with renowned knifemakers, among them such prominent names such as Ernest Emerson, Warren Osborne, and Bob Lum. As unusual as some designs are, a small-format gentleman's folder such as the Megumi (this Japanese name means "blessing" or "benevolence") is rather atypical for Benchmade's range of products.

But Benchmade shines in the professional realization of this pocket knife according to a design of the Japanese Seiichi Nakamura, who also drafted the model Shoki, in 2008, awarded "IWA Knife of the Year." The retired engineer also contributed his own locking mechanism: the so-called Nak-Lok is based on the principle of the liner lock, but in this case the locking liner is not located at the handle's bottom side but at its back, where it latches into a recess of the blade tang. In order to close the knife, you have to press on a bolt that bends the spring backwards so that the blade can be closed again—single-handedly, of course.

Only the finest materials are used for the knife: Benchmade uses high-quality S30V steel for the flat-ground blade. The handle scales are each made of a single piece of carbon fiber flanked by two small strips of cocobolo wood. The decorated handle back is made of a component created in metal spraying technique. Beyond all technical finesse, the Megumi appeals especially with its elegant and unobtrusive appearance.

SPECIFICATIONS

OVERALL LENGTH:	149 mm
BLADE LENGTH:	65 mm
BLADE THICKNESS:	2.5 mm
WEIGHT:	52 g
HANDLE MATERIAL:	carbon fiber/cocobolo
BLADE STEEL:	S30V
LOCKING MECHANISM:	Nak-Lok
WHERE PRODUCED:	United States
WEBSITE:	www.benchmade.com

▸ **CARBON FIBER AND COCOBOLO WOOD:** the combination of a modern material with a traditional one provides an exciting contrast. A pretty detail is the tiny cocobolo disk inlaid in the thumb stud, which can be unscrewed.

The Rise to Beauty

On a February evening in 416 BCE, in the house of tragedian Agathon, the intellectual elite of Athens assembled in order to celebrate the author who had won a literary competition the day before. Among the participants of the banquet were such prominent minds as the philosopher Socrates and Agathon's poet colleague Aristophanes. Since they had already caroused the day before, they decided to limit the consumption of wine and to instead spend the evening with an informal speech competition. Each of the guests should in turn improvise a speech on the god Eros.

Admittedly, this evening banquet never took place as described; it was just an ingenious invention of Plato. In his famous work *Symposion* he puts the various opinions concerning Eros into the mouth of the illustrious guests. The most important speech is held by Socrates, who brings forward the Eros teachings of the mysterious seer Diotima. Here erotic desire at first turns towards the beauty of the body, then to the beauty of activities and knowledge, and finally, at the highest level, sees perfect beauty itself.

A reflection of this beauty is also transmitted by the pocket knife christened Eros, designed by the Hawaiian knifemaker Ken Onion and produced in series by CRKT. With respect to style it unites—using the philosophical jargon again—tactical beauty with gentleman-like beauty. The extremely pointed blade and the flipper give the blade a decidedly tactical appearance; the delicately designed titanium handle scales and the slim construction nevertheless turn the knife into a cultivated everyday companion. Despite its feather-light construction, the frame lock is stable enough for locking the blade reliably. The hollow grind and the stainless Japanese steel Acuto+ provide uncomplicated cutting joy. Fans of technical finesse also get their money's worth, since the Eros is equipped with the IKBS ball bearing system, developed by Rick Lala and Flavio Ikoma. By means of it, the knife can be opened fast as lightning.

With the model Eros, the designer Ken Onion, who has proven himself in many genres, has achieved a definite mix of styles without any fashionable razzle-dazzle.

SPECIFICATIONS

OVERALL LENGTH:	177 mm
BLADE LENGTH:	76 mm
BLADE THICKNESS:	2 mm
WEIGHT:	44 g
HANDLE MATERIAL:	titanium
BLADE STEEL:	Acuto+
LOCKING MECHANISM:	frame lock
WHERE PRODUCED:	Taiwan
WEBSITE:	www.crkt.com

▸ **REAL BEAUTY INSTEAD OF VULGAR SEX APPEAL:** whatever caused Ken Onion to call this pocket knife Eros, the name integrates it into a tradition going along with Plato's insight into the nature of erotic desire: "But Eros is a desire aimed at beauty."

The Joy of Cutting

In the life of every knife enthusiast sooner or later the wish arises to have a knife by Chris Reeve. The person and brand name Chris Reeve have achieved a cult status that can best be compared to that of the mature Steve Jobs and Apple. Many knife aficionados see the model Sebenza as the embodiment of modern pocket knives.

Beyond the hype around the brand, the euphoric enthusiasm for the knives from Boise, Idaho, has its factual reasons. Chris Reeve has set new standards in the serial production of knives with his devotion to precision. No small number of people have first learned from Chris Reeve what a "smooth" blade movement feels like.

Chris Reeve started his career as knifemaker in South Africa. In 1989, he emigrated to the United States because he counted on better chances for success there. Chris Reeve's bond with his African homeland is expressed by the model names of his knives which are words of the Zulu language. "*Mnandi*" means "very pretty" which is an understatement for the gent's folder with the same name. The Mnandi was first introduced in 2001, and since Chris Reeve sees all his knives as "work in progress," this model, too, has experienced minimal modifications over the years. The design of the pocket clip, for example, was slightly re-worked and the blade steel changed from S30V to S35VN.

In contrast to the other folding knives by Chris Reeve, the Mnandi is a two-hand folder. The blade can be opened comfortably by means of a recess on both sides below the rounded blade back. Serrations over a length of about two centimeters serve as a rest for thumb or forefinger. The handle is made of titanium scales decorated with wooden inlays. One of them also makes up the integral lock, designed by Chris Reeve and also known as frame lock. The locking spring latches underneath the blade tang with a solid snap and provides a lock free of any play. Using this handy knife gives you pure joy when cutting, not the least because of its gentle hollow grind. The pocket clip can be relocated and also be removed, if desired.

SPECIFICATIONS

OVERALL LENGTH:	161 mm
BLADE LENGTH:	69 mm
BLADE THICKNESS:	2.3 mm
WEIGHT:	43 g
HANDLE MATERIAL:	titanium/guaiacum
BLADE STEEL:	S30V
LOCKING MECHANISM:	frame lock
WHERE PRODUCED:	United States
WEBSITE:	www.chrisreeve.com

▸ **CONTINUITY IN CHANGE:** since 2001, the Mnandi is the gentleman's knife par excellence in Chris Reeve's program. Every now and then the choice of materials for the handle scales on offer changes. The depicted knife with guaiacum wood is from the year 2007.

"We Design for the Hand"

Like almost no other knife producer, the American company Spyderco has revolutionized the common idea of a folding knife. Some traditionalists still can't warm up to the unusual look of any Spyderco knife. Sal Glesser, founder of the company, in an interview once stated about Spyderco's design philosophy in a brief and concise way: "We design for the hand, not for the eye."

There are classier and more compact gentleman's pocket knives available from Spyderco than the Sage 1. But this model, which has been available for many years, most obviously represents the typical properties of a Spyderco folder: the famous thumb hole in the blade—called "Spydie hole" by fans—enables you to open the blade with one hand by pressing the thumb lightly onto the hole and rotating the blade out of the handle. This blade cut-out is the distinctive trademark of all Spyderco knives (even the fixed blades). The useful pocket clip is another innovation of Spyderco, which later was taken up by many other producers and today belongs to the standard equipment of modern pocket knives. Although the blade's leaf shape is no invention of the Americans, because of its frequent use, it nevertheless developed into a strong recognition value for the brand.

The models of the Sage series are an homage to the young technical history of pocket knives, by dedicating each to a specific locking mechanism. The Sage 1 started with the liner lock, a locking mechanism invented by Michael Walker during the early 1980s, and since then used by many knife producers. Three other models followed provided with Chris Reeve's integral lock, better known as frame lock, the bolt-action lock of Blackie Collins, and the mid-back lock by Al Mar.

The Sage 1 is equipped with handle scales of G-10, on top of which a layer of carbon fiber has been applied. The pocket clip can be relocated to both sides and lets the knife vanish almost completely in your trouser pocket, where you can hardly feel it due to its low weight of less than 100 grams. The flat grind and high-quality S30V steel provide good cutting abilities and high edge retention.

SPECIFICATIONS

OVERALL LENGTH:	181 mm
BLADE LENGTH:	76 mm
BLADE THICKNESS:	3 mm
WEIGHT:	91 g
HANDLE MATERIAL:	G-10/carbon fiber
BLADE STEEL:	S30V
LOCKING MECHANISM:	liner lock
WHERE PRODUCED:	Taiwan
WEBSITE:	www.spyderco.com

▶ **SETTING THE STYLE FOR A MODERN GENERATION OF POCKET KNIVES:** with the opening hole in the blade and the practical pocket clip, Spyderco redefined the folding knife.

Functional Jewelry

The company William Henry, founded by Matthew William Conable and Michael Henry Honack in 1997—the middle names of the founders creating the company's name, over the years has changed from a manufactory for classy gentleman's knives into a lifestyle outfitter of top notch quality. William Henry defines the pocket knife as "functional jewelry for men." Consequently real jewelry for men, cufflinks, fountain pens, and other precious accessories, such as golf divot tools with diamonds, are now offered under the brand name as well. No wonder that a remarkable number of Hollywood stars are among the customers.

So much glamour looks rather intimidating to the ordinary knife enthusiast; the prices have been put-offish from the very beginning. The exquisite materials and the extremely laborious artistic craftsmanship necessary for decorating the knives justify the pricing. But aesthetically the high-end models are not always convincing. The excessive decoration of damascus, gold, jewels, and engravings sometimes move the knives into the area of luxury kitsch.

The knives of the E6 series in contrast, meant as entry level into the world of William Henry, are unobtrusive in a likeable way. The model variants are distinguished by their handle inlays. While the E6-1 is provided with cocobolo and the E6-3 with inlays of carbon fiber, the E6-2 is decorated with inlays of maple burl wood. The expressive pattern of the wood contrasts with the cool, technical look of the fluted handle scales of black anodized aluminum. Since the construction doesn't need additional liners, the knife weighs no more than 35 grams.

But the E6-2 does not only look pretty, but also fulfills its purpose as a cutting tool: the D2 steel is hardened up to 60-62 HRC, which provides extraordinary edge retention. A black coating of tungsten carbide protects the blade against corrosion. The blade movement is very smooth. The button lock system, typical for William Henry, works reliably: the blade is arrested by means of a bolt and can be unlocked easily by means of pressing a button.

SPECIFICATIONS

OVERALL LENGTH:	158 mm
BLADE LENGTH:	70 mm
BLADE THICKNESS:	2.3 mm
WEIGHT:	35 g
HANDLE MATERIAL:	aluminum/maple burl wood
BLADE STEEL:	D2
LOCKING MECHANISM:	button lock
WHERE PRODUCED:	United States
WEBSITE:	www.williamhenry.com

▸ **BEGINNER'S MODEL:** for William Henry standards, the E6-2 is almost spartan. This modesty has positive effects with respect to aesthetics as well as price. The very lightweight knife not only convinces as a stylish representative of the gentleman genre but also as a functional tool.

Cleaning and Maintenance

ABOUT OILING AND SHARPENING

Since a gentleman's knife usually neither has to suffer under adverse climate conditions nor has to permanently perform extreme cutting services, maintenance is reduced to a minimum.

CLEANING AND MAINTAINING THE HANDLE

If the knife is carried in one's trouser pocket without a pouch or pocket clip, by and by lint and dirt particles will accumulate between the liners and/or handle scales. Knives with screwed handle construction can be cleaned best. Here it is not necessary to take the knife completely apart each time. Pipe cleaners have turned out to be helpful. They can be used to clean the inside of riveted handles, too. At spots with difficult access you can also use a spray with compressed air to blow away loose dust particles.

Dirt on handle scales of natural materials such as bone, horn, or wood should be wiped off with a slightly moist cloth without any additional detergent. Dirt on structured G-10 surfaces quite often is especially tenacious and is the more obvious the brighter the material is. Here usually only soap suds and a toothbrush can help. Otherwise modern handle materials don't need any special care.

Handle scales made of wood should be rubbed with oil every few months. Recommended are linseed oil, camellia oil, and the universal oil Ballistol, which is also suitable for blade care.

Ballistol is food safe, eco-friendly, and doesn't resinate. It is offered in bottles, as a spray, in the shape of a pen, and as cloth. Just rub the oil over the wood and let it soak in for a couple of hours exposed to air. Surplus oil can be wiped off with a piece of cloth or a paper towel. Although horn is rather insensitive, it can become dull and tarnished over time. A treatment with oil or petroleum jelly gives new shine to horn scales.

OPTIMIZING THE BLADE MOVEMENT

If it is necessary to oil a sluggishly moving blade, Ballistol is recommended, too, or the multi-tool oil of Victorinox, which is available in small

▶ **CLEANING AND MAINTENANCE SET:** pipe cleaners, Ballistol and, if necessary, a bit of lubricant oil are sufficient to enjoy your pocket knife for many years.

5-milliliter bottles with practical dosage tip and is not only suitable for Victorinox knives. The oil is neutral to taste and smell and fulfills the strict requirements of the NSF-H1 standard for lubricants which can come into contact with food. In addition to Victorinox, Chris Reeve and Benchmade offer lubricants of their own.

If the blade can be taken apart, first all washers and the blade tang have to be cleaned thoroughly. Afterwards a few drops onto the spots around the axis hole where friction occurs are sufficient to restore smooth blade movement. With a riveted knife, the oil is applied as close to the blade axis as possible and distributed by opening and closing the knife several times.

RUST PREVENTION

Even stainless steels can rust in extreme conditions. For a gentleman's pocket knife this is practically not possible with normal use. In general, all blades should be rinsed immediately after contact with saltwater or solutions containing acid and be wiped dry. If, in addition, the blade is rubbed with Ballistol every once in a while, the knife may still be a joy for your great-grandchildren.

The maintenance of blades of carbon steel is a bit more of an effort. A stay in salty sea air or contact with body sweat can quickly lead to rust. Thus it is absolutely necessary to keep blades of carbon steel dry all the time and to oil them regularly. However, the creation of a patina can hardly be avoided and is even a desired effect by fans of carbon steel blades.

Rusty spots on the surface can be removed with polishing paste. In addition to household remedies there are countless commercial products. The wadding polish of the brand "Nevr-Dull" is gentle but nevertheless effective; it can also be used to bring tarnished brass bolsters back to high gloss.

RE-SHARPENING THE BLADE

Even blades of steel with excellent edge retention will become blunt at some time and will have to be re-sharpened. Since a lot of books and websites exist giving detailed manuals and demonstrative videos with respect to this topic (e.g. www.messer-machen.de), a few general tips should be sufficient here.

Under no circumstances should the blades of high-quality pocket knives be re-sharpened with the cheap sharpeners with small grinding wheels such as can be found in many kitchen drawers. The result is no sharp blades but scratched cutting edges. On the other hand, it is not necessary to spend a fortune on Japanese waterstones with six different grit sizes in order to sharpen the blade of a pocket knife every now and then.

Even though many knife enthusiasts have the ambition to get the most out of a given blade steel to be able to even split hair, in the end, such an extreme sharpness is not necessary for the blade of a gentleman's folder. A decent sharpness is sufficient for use. This sharpness is achieved when the blade slides through a sheet of paper without any effort.

For beginners, a sharpening system is recommended that leads to useful results without much training effort. The advantage of such systems is that they support keeping the grinding angle constant. A sharpening set of Lansky, Gatco, or Spyderco's Sharpmaker is absolutely sufficient in most cases. For blades that have been hardened to more than 60 HRC, the additional purchase of appropriate diamond-coated grinding stones is recommended. The purchase of expensive systems such as Edge Pro or Wicked Edge only pays off if you have to sharpen many blades regularly.

You should not wait in principle until the blade is totally blunt. This is valid especially for blades made of very hard steels. They can hardly be brought back to sharpness by laypersons when

▸ **SUITABLE FOR BEGINNERS:** even untrained persons are able to resharpen their knife blades in one go with the Spyderco Sharpmaker. The triangular ceramic rods can be set up at an angle of 30 or 40 degrees. The brass rods are for protecting one's hands. For hard, powder-metallurgical steels, diamond sharpening stones are available optionally. In addition, Spyderco offers especially fine ceramic rods as add-ons, but these are not absolutely necessary for the blade of a gentleman's knife.

the blade is completely worn out. In order to permanently keep a reasonable sharpness for use, the cutting edge should be maintained by regularly drawing it over a ceramics sharpening stone a few times. Quite often even stropping on a leather strop is sufficient.

Whoever is able to sharpen freehand and travels often will appreciate small sharpening stones such as the ones offered by companies like Fällkniven and Spyderco. They are lightweight, flat, and are delivered with a pouch so you can carry them with you everywhere easily.

▸ **FOR HOME AND TRAVEL:** the handy sharpening stones DC3 and DC4 by Fällkniven are provided with a ceramics and a diamond surface.

BACK LOCK

A locking mechanism also called lock back. Here, a spring mounted at the rear handle end lifts a lever supported in the center that in turn latches into a recess of the blade tang with a hammer-like head, thus blocking the blade. In order to unlock it, the lever has to be pressed downwards against the tension of the spring, which is enabled by a recess in the handle's back. Depending on the lever's length, the exposed part is either at the rear end of the handle or at its center (mid-lock). Traditional knives of Solingen instead have a trigger protruding from the handle back.

BACKSPACER

Expression for a piece of metal or plastics located at the rear handle end between the liners or the handle scales thus keeping them apart. The backspacer is sometimes decorated or fluted.

BUTTON LOCK

With this locking mechanism the blade is arrested by means of a spring-mounted bolt with two different diameters. The thicker part of the bolt fits into a recess of the blade tang, thus blocking it in open position. In order to unlock the blade, the bolt is pressed downwards, resulting in the part of the bolt with the smaller diameter releasing the blade tang.

CHOIL

A notch between handle or ricasso and blade which makes sharpening the knife easier.

DETENT BALL

A small metal ball, sometimes also called ball detent, which is pressed into the locking spring of liner lock or frame lock folders. When the blade is closed, it latches onto a corresponding recess in the blade tang thus preventing the knife from opening inadvertently.

FALSE EDGE

Area of the blade back that is ground, but blunt. The false edge usually starts at the blade tip and goes backwards a couple of centimeters. The false edge is often mixed up with the ricasso.

FIBER

Short for vulcanized fiber, a compound material based on cellulose and known since 1855. This material, which is available in many different colors, is used as a decorative layer between handle scales and liners of pocket knives.

FLAT GRIND

V-shaped grind that starts either directly at the blade back or below it. If the flat grind continues downwards to the cutting edge without a secondary bevel, it is called Scandinavian grind. The blade is then ground "to zero."

FLIPPER

Opening aid used for the first time by American knifemaker Harold "Kit" Carson. It is a nose-shaped blade extension. With the closed knife, the flipper protrudes above the blade back in the area of the blade axis. The knife is opened with sweeping forefinger pressure on the flipper. In open position of the knife, the flipper acts as a finger guard.

FOLDER

Short for folding knife.

FRAME LOCK

Locking mechanism, also known as integral lock, with a springy, movable latch of titanium or stainless steel being part of the handle half. As with the liner lock, the locking spring slips behind the blade tang, thus arresting it. To unlock the blade, the spring is pushed back with the thumb.

FRICTION FOLDER

With folding knives of this construction, the blade is only constrained by friction at the axis and the handle scales. Some friction folders have a prolonged tang that reaches beyond where the blade is attached to the handle. In open position of the knife it is pressed onto the handle back by thumb or forefinger. There is no spring or other safety mechanism.

GUILLOCHE

Artistic manual decoration of watches, jewelry, and knives. Here, decorative patterns are engraved by means of files and other tools. With very elaborately finished pocket knives the liners and blade back are decorated as well.

[I'm not happy with this definition. The author mixes up filework with engravings made with other tools. Guilloche is the art of engraving repetitive and very delicate line patterns. Work done with files is never called engraving.]

HOLLOW GRIND

Also called concave grind because the flanks of the blade are curving inwards to a certain extent. Blades with hollow grind have very good cutting abilities because the blade can slice into the things to be cut without much effort. But due to the large removal of material they are less stable than convexly ground blades.

IKBS

Abbreviation for Ikoma Korth Bearing System, a ball bearing system for pocket knives invented by Flavio Ikoma and Rick Lala.

LANYARD

Aid in drawing the knife or as a safety cord.

LEVER LOCK

Locking mechanism with traditional switchblades. Here a lever lifts a bolt that is under pressure from a spring, thus blocking the blade. The blade is flipped out by means of a second spring in the handle's interior. To prevent triggering the mechanism inadvertently, the lever can be folded over forwards. In order to unlock the mechanism, the locking bolt is lifted again with the lever and the blade pressed out of the handle against the resistance of the flipping spring.

LINER

Liners are thin metal frames that make up the supporting structure of a folder's handle. Handle scales and bolsters are mounted on their outside. As an alternative, the liners can be put into recesses on the insides of the handle scales. In order to keep the weight low, steel liners are frequently "skeletonized," which means that they are provided with drill holes and cutouts. With traditional pocket knives, the liners are usually made of brass; with modern knives they are made of titanium, stainless steel, or aluminum. But handle constructions without any liners exist as well.

LINER LOCK

Locking mechanism for which a springy, moveable part of the liner is used as an arresting spring. This part slips behind the blade tang when the knife is opened and thus arrests the blade. To unlock the blade, the liner is pushed back with the thumb. In contrast to the frame lock, the locking half of the handle consists of two parts (handle scale and liner).

NAIL NICK

A notch underneath the blade back, also called nail groove—especially when it is very long. Here the thumb nail can slip in to open the blade. Sometimes it is also worked as a slot-like hole in the blade.

OPEN FRAME

Handle construction with liner lock and frame lock pocket knives with both handle halves only screwed together by spacers. The handle back is open, which makes cleaning the knife easier.

PRIMARY BEVEL

See *Secondary Bevel*.

RICASSO

The unsharpened area of the blade between cutting edge and handle.

SAN MAI

Japanese expression for a blade composed of three layers with a hard central cutting layer and softer outer layers.

SCANDINAVIAN GRIND

See *Flat Grind*.

SECONDARY BEVEL

Most blades are ground in such a way that they have a primary and a secondary bevel. The primary bevel is the main grind (e. g. hollow grind); the secondary bevel is the cutting edge, set off from the primary bevel by a change in angle. With the Scandinavian grind the secondary bevel is dispensed with.

SHARPNESS FOR EVERYDAY USE

This expression is not exactly defined but describes an acceptable sharpness distinct from razor sharpness. If a blade is able to cleanly cut through a sheet of paper, it generally has an acceptable sharpness for everyday use.

SLIPJOINT

A folder construction of the seventeenth century with a back spring holding the knife in open position. The blade is not locked in this position.

SPHERICAL GRIND

Also called convex grind. Here the flanks of the blade are slightly curved outwards, but quite often only the proximity of the cutting edge is shaped convexly.

STONEWASH FINISH

A surface treatment with the individual components (blade, handle scales, pocket clip, etc.) "washed" together with small pebble-shaped abrasive compounds in a drum. Depending on shape and size of the abrasive compounds, the finish looks different. The fine pattern of scratches lets the scratches created later by use look less obvious.

SUMINAGASHI

A suminagashi blade is provided with a central cutting layer of hard steel. Several layers of damascus are added on both flanks of the blade.

TANG

Extended part of the blade fixed to the knife handle. With folders, this is the part where the axis hole is located and where the locking mechanism grips.

THUMB DISK

A small disk-like piece of metal or plastic attached to the blade back that can be used as a thumb stud. With most folders the thumb disk can be unscrewed.

THUMB STUD

Opening aid, also called thumb pin, which enables single-handed opening of the knife with the thumb. Thumb studs can be mounted on one or both sides of the blade. With some knives, the thumb stud can be screwed off, if necessary.

WASHERS

Thin rings of nylon, Teflon, copper, or phosphorous bronze that decrease the friction between blade tang and liners.

ALL IMAGES, WITH THE EXCEPTION OF THE ONES LISTED BELOW, WERE PROVIDED BY THE AUTHOR.

▸ **Page 11:** Roman "Swiss Army Knife," The Fitzwilliam Museum, Cambridge.

▸ **Page 11 (top):** folder sixth century, Wikimedia Commons (http:// commons. wikimedia.org/wiki/File:Folding_knife_6th_century.jpg).

▸ **Page 11 (bottom):** Viking knife ninth century, Deutsches Klingenmuseum (German Blade Museum), Solingen.

▸ **Page 13:** reproduction of the item in the French National Library, Paris.

▸ **Pages 15, 16, 18, 19 (bottom):** Prints courtesy of the Egginton Group, Sheffield.

▸ **Page 19 (top):** I*XL pocket knife, Ken Spielvogel, Sardinia, Ohio.

▸ **Page 20:** catalog page, Taylor's Eye Witness, Sheffield.

▸ **Page 22:** Daniel Peres, collection Franz Hendrichs, Solingen.

▸ **Page 24:** Lieferfrauen (delivery women), city archive Solingen.

▸ **Page 29 (left):** Northfield Pocket Knives, unknown source.

▸ **Page 29 (right):** patent no. 36.321, United States Patent Office.

▸ **Page 30:** back lock folder, Queen Cutlery, Titusville, Pennsylvania.

▸ **Pages 31, 32:** John Russell Case and Case logo, W.R. Case & Sons, Bradford, Pennsylvania.

▸ **Page 33:** group photos, Queen Cutlery, Titusville, Pennsylvania.

▸ **Page 35:** Adolph Kastor and Camillus workers, collection David Anthony.

▸ **Pages 41, 45:** Raffir, Hadsten, Denmark (photographer: Ib Dyhr).

▸ **Page 54:** Damasteel, Söderfors, Sweden.

▸ **Page 68:** Laguiole en Aubrac, Espalion.

▸ **Page 69:** Passion France, Darmstadt.

▸ **Pages 71, 72:** Forge de Laguiole, Laguiole.

▸ **Page 76:** Coltelleria Saladini, Scarperia.

▸ **Pages 78–80:** Coltelleria Berti, Saladini, and ConAz, Scarperia.

▸ **Page 86:** catalog page, collection David Anthony.

▸ **Page 89 (left):** Ka-Bar, Olean, New York.

▸ **Page 90:** W.R. Case & Sons, Bradford, Pennsylvania.